*Artists and Writers in
the Evolution of Latin America*

ARTISTS AND WRITERS

IN

THE EVOLUTION OF LATIN AMERICA

EDITED BY
EDWARD DAVIS TERRY

*Published for the Latin American
Studies Program, University of Alabama*
by
UNIVERSITY OF ALABAMA PRESS
University, Alabama

PREFACE

Except for two, the articles in this volume are based on papers given at the XV Annual Southeastern Conference on Latin American Studies (SECOLAS) held at the University of Alabama from April 4th to the 6th, 1968. The theme for the conference was "The Role of Artists, Thinkers, and Writers in the Evolution of Latin America."

Grateful acknowledgment is given to the authors for permission to publish their articles and to the Office for International Programs, University of Alabama, for making it possible to publish this volume.

I want to express my sincere appreciation to the following people for their editorial assistance: Ruy Alencar, Iredell Jenkins, Jay Murphy, James M. Salem, Alvin C. Sella, Bernardo Suárez, James O. Swain, and Alfred B. Thomas. Special thanks are due to Hubert E. Mate for his considerable aid and advice on the articles from Brazil.

Edward Davis Terry

CONTRIBUTORS

LUIZ FRANCO DE SA BACELLAR of Manaus, Amazonas, Brazil, won the National Award for Poetry "Flauta de Barro," Rio de Janeiro, 1965.

RAY F. BROUSSARD is Associate Professor of Latin American history, University of Georgia.

FLORENE J. DUNSTAN is Chairman of the Department of Spanish, Agnes Scott College, Decatur, Georgia.

JOHN E. ENGLEKIRK is Professor of Spanish and Portuguese at the University of California at Los Angeles and currently a member of the Executive Committee of the Instituto Internacional de Literatura Iberoamericana.

ROBERTO ESQUENAZI-MAYO is Director of the Institute for Latin American and International Studies at the University of Nebraska.

FEDERICO G. GIL is Kenan Professor of Political Science, Research Professor in the Institute for Research in Social Science, and Director of the Institute of Latin American Studies at the University of North Carolina, Chapel Hill.

JOHN H. HADDOX is head of the Department of Philosophy, University of Texas at El Paso.

OYAMA CESAR ITUASSU DA SILVA is Professor of International Law and Dean of the Faculty of Law, Universidade do Amazonas, Manaus, Brazil.

MARIO YPIRANGA MONTEIRO is Professor of Brazilian and Portuguese Literature in the Faculty of Philosophy, Sciences, and Letters at the Universidade do Amazonas, Manaus, Brazil.

FRANCISCO MONTERDE is President of the Academia Mexicana de la Lengua, Mexico City.

EDWARD H. MOSELEY is Assistant Professor of Latin American history at the University of Alabama.

RICHARD A. PRETO-RODAS is Assistant Professor of Portuguese in the Department of Foreign Languages, University of Florida.

DANIEL R. REEDY of the University of Kentucky, is Associate Professor of Spanish in the Department of Spanish and Italian.

JOHN L. VOGT, JR. is Assistant Professor of History at the University of Georgia, Athens.

LESTER C. WALKER, JR. is Professor of Art at the University of Georgia, Athens.

CONTENTS

Introduction
Edward Davis Terry

Philosophy and Government

ARTISTS AND WRITERS

IN

THE EVOLUTION OF LATIN AMERICA

Introduction

Edward Davis Terry

Introduction

ARTISTS AND WRITERS have played an active and an important role in contemporary Latin American society (e.g., Rómulo Gallegos of Venezuela, Guillermo Leon Valencia of Colombia, Diego Rivera of Mexico, and Miguel Angel Asturias of Guatemala), and have done so since the beginning of the Spanish conquest. The "intellectuals" have always exerted more influence on the development of political, religious, and social institutions in the Spanish- and Portuguese-speaking nations to the south than has been the case in the United States. Often, presidents or prominent generals who were primarily professional men of arms or diplomats were recognized by literary critics as great writers, thinkers, and fine literary stylists (e.g., Bolívar and Sarmiento).

An excellent example of the early soldier-writer in Latin America is Hernán Cortés (1485–1547), a bold, courageous, and brilliant military leader. Cortés was the first chronicler of the conquest of Mexico with his *Cartas de relación*. In his *Carta segunda* to Charles V, he gave a colorful and detailed account of his meeting with Moctezuma II before the Aztec capital of Tenochtitlán. Cortés is very readable today because his fresh and vigorous style makes his extraordinary exploits come alive, and his clear prose is often compared to Caesar's *Commentaries*.

A controversial figure during the early colonial period, Fray Bartolomé de las Casas (1474–1565) wrote and preached

1

tirelessly in defense of the Indians who were being extermi-
nated in the Antilles and enslaved throughout the Spanish
empire in the New World. Although Las Casas wrote his
chronicles as part of his defense of the Indians, one finds interesting novelistic accounts scattered through his works,
such as the story of the rebellion of Enriquillo in Santo Domingo.

The conquest in South America inspired Alonso de Ercilla
y Zúñiga (1533–1594), a courtier and soldier of Philip II, to
write *La araucana*, an epic portraying the heroism and tenacity of the Araucanian Indians in Chile in their fight against the
invading Spaniards. This work, written partly by campfire
during campaigns, is generally considered by literary critics to
be the finest learned epic in the Spanish language.

A contemporary of Ercilla, the Inca Garcilaso de la Vega
(1539–1616) occupied a unique position in colonial Peru. His
father was a cousin of the talented Castilian poet and cavalier
Garcilaso de la Vega, and his mother was an Incan princess
who reared him in the customs of her people. Thus the Inca
Garcilaso was prepared, as no one else, to interpret authori-
tatively the civilization of his maternal ancestors, and he did
so in his colorful and highly readable *Comentarios reales que
tratan del origen de los Incas* (1609). His *La Florida del Inca*
(1605), which reads like a romance of adventure, is an account of the explorations of Hernando de Soto.

The historical development of Brazil has been similar to
that of other Latin American nations, and especially from
1580 to 1640, when Portugal was governed by the Spanish
monarch.

The Jesuits wielded tremendous influence in colonial Brazil through the schools which they founded for the education
of the Indians. Father José de Anchieta (1530–1597) was a
philologist who composed hymns, songs, and grammars in
Portuguese, Spanish, Latin, and Tupí, thereby laying the
foundations of spiritual and social unity in Brazil.

In the seventeenth century, Father Antônio Vieira (1608–1697), brought to Brazil as a child, became one of the outstanding orators and prose writers in the Portuguese language. He defended Brazil against abuses by governors and European merchants, and he also advocated the abolition of slavery.

José Bonifácio de Andrada e Silva (1765–1838) was an orator, poet, and scientist. Called the father of Brazilian independence, he was esteemed as the most learned man in Brazil in sciences (his specialization was mineralogy) and letters.

Painting reached artistic heights in colonial Spanish America in the seventeenth and eighteenth centuries. José Ibarra (1688–1756) was called the Mexican Murillo, and Miguel de Santiago (? – 1673) of Quito was known as the Apelles of America.

Sculpture in colonial Mexico was almost always done by anonymous artists and was religious in motif. Manuel Tolsá (1757–1815), who created in the eighteenth century the famous equestrian statue of Charles IV in Mexico City, was the first prominent sculptor in Mexico.

Quito was the site of the most renowned school of sculpture in colonial America. Two of the outstanding artists of this school were Indians, Manuel Chili (eighteenth century)—called "Caspicara"—who did group sculpture, and Gaspar Zangurima (eighteenth century), an architect, painter, and sculptor with many followers.

Art in colonial Brazil was distinguished especially for religious architecture, which was generally influenced by the Portuguese Baroque style. Antônio Francisco Lisboa (1730–1814), called "o Aleijadinho" (the Little Cripple), was a fine architect and one of the greatest sculptors in colonial America. His work can still be admired in almost all the churches in the state of Minas Gerais.

Latin America has a rich musical background dating back

to pre-Columbian times. Beginning with the Conquest the native music combined with the European and African to produce original and varied compositions. During colonial times composers of note were found in Peru, Brazil, Venezuela, Cuba, and Mexico. For example, Father Pedro Palacios Sojo (1739–1799) and José Angel Lamas (? –1814) were active composers in Venezuela in the eighteenth century.

Writers continued to play an active part in the society of the late colonial period and in the independence movement in the Latin American colonies. José Joaquín Fernández de Lizardi (1776–1827) was an avid supporter of the Mexican struggle for freedom. He founded the newspaper *El Pensador Mexicano* in order to have a means of circulating his revolutionary propaganda. When his newspaper was suppressed, Lizardi continued his incisive criticism of the colonial government and society in his picaresque novel *El periquillo Sarniento*, the first novel in Spanish America. Fernández de Lizardi was the most forceful propagandist of independence and also the most important literary figure in Mexico during the first third of the nineteenth century.

Many South American writers worked untiringly for freedom and afterwards for stable governments. José Joaquín Olmedo (1780–1847) of Ecuador, the author of the heroic poem "La Victoria de Junín: Canto a Bolívar," dedicated a large part of his life to the service of his country. In 1811 he went to Spain to represent Guayaquil in the Cortes of Cádiz, returning home in 1814 to take an important part in the independence movements of Ecuador and Peru. Olmedo himself in 1823 carried the petition of Peru to Bolívar, which requested help against the Spaniards. After independence had been won, Olmedo went to Europe as a special envoy of Bolívar. In later years he became active in Ecuadorian politics and was a candidate for the presidency in 1845.

Another dedicated revolutionary, Andrés Bello (1781–

1865) of Venezuela and later of Chile, was the most erudite scholar in Latin America during the nineteenth century. Bello played an important role in the South American independence movement, going to London in 1810 as a revolutionary agent and remaining there in that capacity until 1829. His influence became more extensive in 1826 with the founding of his journal, *El repertorio americano* (1826–1828), in which he defended the cause of liberty and independence and published literary and cultural material that he hoped would draw the widely separated Spanish American states closer together culturally. Bello was the principal author of the Civil Code of Chile (1855), and he also wrote one of the first important treatises on international law.

Simón Bolívar (1783–1830), known as the Liberator and as the George Washington of South America, is often overlooked as a writer. The "thinker of the Revolution" displayed a clear and direct style in his letters (e.g., *Letter from Jamaica*), speeches, and other political writings. It is obvious from these writings that Bolívar was a writer of great merit, and had he not been so busy with the task of securing independence for his own and neighboring countries, he could have achieved widespread recognition in a career in letters.

The author who introduced Romanticism into Argentina, Esteban Echeverría (1805–1851), lived a romantic and active political life, and resided for four years (1826–1830) in Paris, a stronghold of Romanticism. In 1832 Echeverría published his long poem *Elvira o la novia del Plata*, the first romantic work in Argentine literature. Echeverría was very active in efforts to overthrow the dictator Juan Manuel de Rosas, and to that end he founded the *Asociación de mayo* in 1837. In 1840 he had to go into exile in Montevideo in order to escape the agents of Rosas. Echeverría's "El matadero" is a realistic short story and is a blistering indictment, in parts almost nauseating, of Rosas' cruel and bloody regime.

One of the Argentine literati most dedicated to the overthrow of Rosas was José Mármol (1816–1871). In 1839 he was thrown into prison by Rosas but supposedly continued to write caustic verses against the tyrant on the walls of his jail. On being freed, Mármol went to Montevideo, a haven for Argentines in exile, in order to continue his campaign against the dictatorship. He had to flee to Rio de Janeiro later when the Argentine army invaded Uruguay. Mármol's novel *Amalia* (1851, 1855), the first novel in Argentina, describes Buenos Aires during the time of Rosas, and the omnipresent terror of Rosas pervades the atmosphere of *Amalia* as it did that of Buenos Aires for almost twenty years.

Argentina has produced many outstanding figures through the years. One of the most illustrious was Domingo Faustino Sarmiento (1811–1888), an extraordinary man endowed with many talents. He rose from a humble background to excel as a writer, statesman, and educator, and to become President of Argentina (1868–1874). Sarmiento was self-educated, having little formal schooling, but his collected writings make up fifty-two volumes dealing with educational, political, and sociological topics. His *Facundo o civilización y barbarie* (1845) is the outstanding prose work in Argentina during the nineteenth century.

Sarmiento served as ambassador to the United States, which he ardently admired for her tradition of freedom and liberty. He arrived in May 1865 and became a friend of leaders in various fields, including Horace Mann—whose wife later translated Sarmiento's *Facundo* into English. While on a ship returning to Argentina in 1868, Sarmiento learned that, in absentia, he had been elected President, an honor which pointed up the respect of his compatriots for him.

José Martí (1853–1895), the Cuban *Apóstol de la libertad*, was another happy blend of writer and statesman. He was a prolific writer and an excellent poet. He lived much of his life outside Cuba, in exile, and his literary and political influence spread throughout Latin America. Martí was obsessed with the idea of independence for Cuba. Not only for his literary, political, and social writings but also for his life and his interest in the freedom of man, will he be forever an apostle of liberty to Cubans and to all who may be oppressed in Latin America.

Ecuador contributed another foe of tyranny in Juan Montalvo (1832–1889), who hated all dictators. In his journal *El cosmopolita* (1866–1869) he bitterly attacked his own country's despot, García Moreno, to the point that he had to go into exile. While in exile in 1875, he received news of the assassination of García Moreno. It is told that he exclaimed, "¡Mi pluma le ha matado!" Because of continued differences with the government, Montalvo was exiled permanently from Ecuador and lived in Panama and France. His famous *Siete tratados* was written about 1873 but was published later in France in 1882.

One of Peru's greatest literary figures is Ricardo Palma (1833–1919). Palma was born in Lima and was a resident there for most of his life. He created the *tradición*, which is recognized as a new literary genre—the historical anecdote. During the War of the Pacific (1879–1883) Chilean troops destroyed Palma's house and sacked and plundered the Biblioteca Nacional. After the war the government gave him the task of rebuilding the Biblioteca Nacional's fine collection. He attracted donations of books from many parts of the world, and he also succeeded in regaining many works from Chile.

A few eminent Latin American writers have had political and cultural influence throughout the Western Hemisphere. Such was José Enrique Rodó (1872–1917) of Uruguay, an essayist and scholar, who participated in the national life as director of the Biblioteca Nacional and later as a member of the Chamber of Deputies. *Ariel* (1900), Rodó's first and most famous work, has had a tremendous influence on United States-Latin American relations. In it he urged that a small, aristocratic society in Latin America endeavor to counteract the materialistic influence of the United States, and he contrasted, in a careful analysis, the North American society with the Latin American, insisting, however, that the two civilizations can work together and complement each other.

In the nineteenth century Brazil gave the world two men of letters of the highest rank: Joaquim Maria Machado de Assis (1839–1908) and Euclides da Cunha (1866–1909). Machado de Assis was a great creator of characters and a keen, often ironical, psychological analyst (*Memórias Póstumas de Brás Cubas*, 1880). Da Cunha is internationally known for his *Os Sertões* (1902), translated by Samuel Putman in 1944 as *Rebellion in the Backlands*. It is an account of life in the arid northeast and of the inhabitants' heroic resistance in 1896–1897 at the siege of Canudos.

Except in Brazil and Chile, the nineteenth century in Latin America was hardly favorable to cultural activities, as a result of the generally unstable times. There was no longer much demand for sculpture and painting for churches; as a result, these arts declined in importance. Many painters, such as Juan Cordero (1824–1884) in Mexico and Prilidiano Pueyrrendón (1823–1870) of Argentina, turned to landscape and historical scenes. In Lima, Pancho Fierro (1803–1879) specialized in watercolors of folk life. In Uruguay, Juan Manuel Blanes (1830–1901) painted as his favorite subject the countryside around the Río de la Plata. Pedro Figari (1861–1938), also of Uruguay and one of the most important artists of the Americas, depicted with an exquisite sense of color South American landscape scenes.

The outstanding nineteenth-century composer in Latin America was Carlos Gomes (1836–1896) of Brazil, who had nine operas produced in Europe and America. His best known work is *O Guaraní* (La Scala, Milan, 1870), whose score is influenced by Verdi's *Aïda*.

By the late nineteenth and early twentieth centuries Latin American literature ranked with the best in world literature but was slow in receiving recognition of its merits. Worldwide recognition became a reality in the honors bestowed upon Gabriela Mistral (1889–1957), a Chilean elementary school teacher and educator, who became Latin America's first Nobel Prize winner in 1945, receiving the Nobel Prize for Literature. As early as 1922 she had won international fame as an educator, and in that year she went to Mexico to aid José Vasconcelos in that country's educational reforms. In her later years Gabriela Mistral became an international cultural and diplomatic representative for her country in Europe, Mexico, Brazil, and the United States.

The Mexican Revolution of 1910 has unique importance in the evolution of Latin America because it was the first revolution to bring about social change. The social and economic phases of the Revolution are still going on today. It has greatly influenced all aspects of life in Mexico and Latin America, and the cultural life has been no exception. A physician-novelist, Mariano Azuela (1873–1952), wrote the novel (*Los de abajo*, 1915) that set in motion an entire cycle of novels dealing with the violent aspects of the Revolution and its aftermath, and their influence spread throughout Spanish America. The articles on Mexican art and on José Vasconcelos illustrate well the important influence that the Revolution had on art, education, and other facets of life in Mexico after the conflict.

Miguel Angel Asturias (1899–   ) of Guatemala, one of the greatest writers in Spanish today, received the Nobel Prize for Literature in 1967. His novels, strongly influenced by Mayan traditions and national themes, treat of the social, political, and economic problems of Guatemala and Central

America, many of which are common to all Latin America.

In Brazil Érico Veríssimo (1905–   ), a much translated novelist, and Gilberto Freyre (1900–   ), a well-known essayist and sociologist, are internationally famous and influential.

Today Latin American artists are recognized as ranking with the best in the world. José Sabogal (1888–   ) of Peru specializes in indigenous themes, whereas Jesús Soto (1923–   ) of Venezuela is interested in representing movement in space, and sometimes uses plexiglass, wire, and steel to gain his effects. Mexico has given the world some of its greatest muralists in Diego Rivera (1887–1957), José Clemente Orozco (1883–1949), and David Alfaro Siqueiros (1898–   ). Their paintings depict scenes with historical, political, and social themes and in some instances were centers of controversy.

In recent years sculpture has made use of new motifs. The Peruvian Joaquín Roca Rey (1923–   ), working with metals, has produced decorative works of charming harmony. In Argentina Rogelio Yrurtia (1879–   ), still using classic style, has wrought several monuments in Buenos Aires.

During the twentieth century, Brazil has become one of the most important contributors to world art. For example, Cândido Portinari (1903–1962) is considered one of the greatest artists of the century. He was a vigorous painter with a strong sense of social responsibility and is lauded for his murals (Rio de Janeiro, Washington, D.C., and the United Nations building).

Contemporary musicians in Latin America, both composers and performers, are among the most talented and imaginative in the world. Brazil's Heitor Villa-Lobos (1887–1959), a prolific creator of varied compositions, is one of the outstanding composers. He was described by the Spanish musicologist Adolfo Salazar as possessing "mental agility and creative spontaneity."

Carlos Chávez (1899–   ) of Mexico has evolved in his compositions from nationalism to what he calls "universalism." Two of his several well-known works are *The New Fire* (1921) and *Invention for Piano* (1958). Diego Rivera collaborated with Chávez in the production of his ballet *H. P.* (*Horsepower*, 1926–1927). Chávez was invited to deliver the Charles Eliot Norton Lectures at Harvard University in 1960–1961. In 1968 he received the annual Koussevitzky Prize awarded by the Swiss government, "for the recording of his six symphonies made by Columbia Records of New York."

It is apparent from this brief discussion that writers and artists have played, and still are playing, an important role in molding the political, educational, religious, and cultural aspects of Latin American life. Usually they have also had to have other careers in order to make a living, and through those careers have exerted important influences on their contemporary society. Also, the man or woman of culture in Latin America has traditionally commanded much respect at all levels of society. Consequently, those admired and respected have tended to enter actively into public life in order to create a society after their particular ideals. The people were and are willing to accept them as leaders and have made it possible for a great number of cultured Latin Americans to rise to high positions in public life, and occasionally to the presidency itself.

ARTISTS AND WRITERS

IN

THE EVOLUTION OF LATIN AMERICA

Literature of Social Protest

John E. Englekirk

Miguel Angel Asturias:
"¡Mejor llamarlas novelas! ..."

M Y TEXT IS taken from the epigraph of *Week-end en Guatemala*:

> ¿No ve las cosas que pasan? . . .
> ¡Mejor llamarlas novelas! . . .[1]

Asturias had served under Arbenz as his ambassador from 1945 until the overthrow of the regime in 1954 when Colonel Carlos Castillo Armas invaded Guatemala with the aid of mercenaries and, allegedly, the support of the U.S. The invasion in itself read like comic opera: the secrecy of its beginnings and development, the charges and countercharges, the brutality of the uneven struggle, and the blitz-like character of its dénouement were incredible to the point of sheer mockery of the truth. To cap it all, the rumors and accusations that the CIA had engineered the entire affair from Panama, with the connivance of other mid-American satellite states, was even more than Sergeant Peter Harkins could swallow—drunk as he was at a Brooklyn bar where he tried to recall the fantastic weekend he had spent as a "tourist" involved in smuggling arms from an air-delivered cache on the Pacific shore to a secret base of operations of the "liberacionistas" in the highlands. Harkins was unable to explain how he could have "lost" the entire truckload on the hard overnight run to the base. When he insisted that he had not been drinking to excess, the Ambassador angrily reminded

him that "we are at war." "At war," popped Peter's eyes in-
credulously. "With whom, Russia?" "No, Sergeant Harkins,
don't act stupid. We are at war with this country, and you are
drunk!" Sergeant could only reply: "Yes, Mr. Ambassador, I
am drunk, because if you say that we are at war with this
miniature republic, then, sir, I *am borracho, totalmente borracho.*" And through big, burly Peter Harkins, who was from
California, probably a graduate of Stanford, a journalist and
globe-trotter, and something of a poet who had come out of
World War II "durmiendo un sueño sin sueños,"[2] Asturias
spoke out for millions of incredulous ones everywhere when
he stuttered his disbelief: "Sólo borracho podía creer que mi
país, el país más poderoso del mundo, pudiera estar en guerra
con un país tan pequeño, tan inofensivo . . . ¡ja . . . ja . . . ja! . . .
era una vergüenza y había que estar total, absoluta, com-
pletamente borracho, y seguir así, para creerlo . . . borracho
. . . borracho de caerse. . . ." (p. 16)[3]

Had he chosen to do so, Asturias, too, could have launched
a series of direct open protests against the international move
to thwart his government's drive for agrarian reform. Juan
José Arévalo, Luis Cardoza y Aragón, and other liberals, all
equally facile with the pen, had crowded the press with accusations that the doubters would dismiss as blatant propaganda. After all, who was so naïve as to believe the "trumped-
up charges" and "facts" that mushroomed out of the inglorious
affair! So once again Asturias turned to fiction as a more re-
liable instrument for reporting and condemning a situation
that could only be described in terms of "una visión de borracho." Chained with his guilt to a bar in Brooklyn: "¡Con-
denada cosa estar en Brooklyn!", Sergeant Harkins provides
the leitmotif and title for the first of the eight "novelas," or
episodes, that summarize the events and the consequences of
his fantastic weekend in Guatemala, all the more fantastic
for the Sergeant, because had he not been a war hero of the
Normandie invasion, he would most certainly have been ac-

cused of complicity with the enemy! No, the only way to report so incredible an event was to portray it as the product of the madness and absurdity of a world of fiction.

The other tales are patterned after this key theme. Peter Harkins, the "tourist," returned from his "blitz weekend" to pay the price for his innocent participation in a disgraceful act perpetrated, presumably, by an amoral government agency. But other Americans—like those of the story that follows, "¡Americanos todos!"—would continue to come, albeit on the more traditional tour, in search of quaint customs and costumes still cherished by an "illiterate and backward folk."

Milocho, the popular guide, can no longer suffer the blood-stained presence of the "ladies and gentlemen" of his tour. He sees them now as so many accomplices of the "assassins" who had ruthlessly bombed his helpless countrymen and his beautiful land. Milocho counts the "barbarians" in the rear vision mirror of the bus as they start out for Lago Atitlán; there are 29 of them . . . 29 . . . 29, exactly the number of his own *paisanos* who had been shot at "Nagualcachita" by a colonel of their own armed forces as the "pacification" movement got under way. When Milocho tells of the destruction caused over the years by the volcanoes Agua and Fuego and Acatenango, he explains these natural phenomena as acts of vengeance on the part of the gods for "las crueldades de los que diezmaban las poblaciones indígenas, ahorcaban a sus caciques, humillaban a sus gentes. . . ."[4] Alarica Powell, the "golondrina rubia" from California, his erstwhile sweetheart, comments in reply: "¡Eso era antes, darling, eso era antes, ahora los volcanes son como ustedes. . . . No sirven para nada!" (p. 57)[5] And the mockery of her remarks keep pounding through Milocho's mind: "eso era antes . . . eso era antes . . . para nada . . . para nada . . . ," until he plunges them all to their death, Alarica, himself and all the 29—"¡Americanos . . . americanos todos . . . !" (p. 60)

There were enemies also from within: the church, the

landed aristocracy, the fruit interests, all those who opposed
agrarian reform, and even the army that had betrayed the
government and the people's cause when the big gringo
planes fresh from Korea hurled death on the long-suffering
ones below. As loyal Valeria in "Ocelotle 33" explains to her
little sons, who jump out of bed to do battle with the mysterious and dangerous beast, operation "Ocelotle 33": "No, mis
hombrecitos, no . . . el Ocelotle 33 ya se ha ido . . . fue una
pesadilla y de las pesadillas, se despierta. . . ." And then to
herself, half-choked with tears, she added: "De las pesadillas
se despierta, pero no de la realidad. De la realidad, no hay
quien despierte." (p. 76)[6]

In "La Galla" anyone remotely associated with agrarian reform is blacklisted as a communist. And so it was that even
the leader of the Cofradía Grande, Diego Hun Ig, was labelled "el cabecilla comunista," and one of his daughters
was outraged by the foreman of the road gang who wanted
to teach her the meaning of free love—"eso que tu padre
proclamaba . . . tener hijos para el estado." (p. 88)[7] . . . The
disillusionment of the twice dispossessed is the theme of "El
Bueyón." Their newly acquired "tierrecitas" vanish suddenly,
as if in a dream—"¡Sí, un sueño que como fuego prendido en
el descampado, se apagó pronto!"—to fall once again into
the hands of foreigners who would continue to be "dueños de
nuestra miseria, de nuestra ruina, de nuestra pobreza. . . ."

> —¡Fue un sueño, Nana Caida!
> —Sí, un sueño. . . . (p. 96)[8]

And in "Los Agrarios" Asturias focuses on still another facet
of the problem of land reform. Wrested of his vast holdings,
Don Félix bursts into a frenzied fit of mockery over the im-
potence of the agrarians when pitted in open conflict with
their multiheaded enemy:

> Ciento sesenta millones de gringos y gringas y gringuitos y
> gringotes . . . ¡ja . . . ja! la compañía más poderosa de la órbita

del Caribe . . . ¡ja . . . ja! . . . la iglesia católica de Nueva York, del país y del mundo entero . . . ¡ja . . . ja! . . . tres Presidentes de tres Repúblicas, por lo menos, ¡ja . . . ja! . . . cadenas de periódicos y agencias noticiosas . . . ¡ja . . . ja! . . . armas automáticas último modelo . . . ¡ja . . . ja! . . . cataratas de dólares, bombarderos, jefes militares de alta graduación listos para entregarse al ver que la cosa se pone a favor nuestro . . . y un ejército alquilado . . . ¡ja . . . ja . . . ! Tiburcio Sotoj . . . Guadalupe Sotoj . . . Rufino Sotoj . . . ¡ja . . . ja! . . . contra ese menú de casa rica qué podrán ustedes los agrarios . . . ¡ja . . . ja . . . ja . . . ja! . . . (pp. 151–152)[9]

Don Félix was right; who could long prevail against so formidable a foe! But a shower of agrarian bullets suddenly cuts short his mocking laughter.

Again, in "¡Cadáveres para la publicidad!," Asturias recaptures yet another aspect of "las cosas que pasan" when he relates how the "Master" publicity man, especially brought down from New York to win the people over to the new "Coronel-gobierno de Liberación," whips up a propaganda campaign based on the slogan "Corpses, corpses, corpses"— "Mejor en inglés que en español. . . . En inglés la palabra tenía un raro sonido de picotazo o grito de ave de rapiña"— corpses, corpses, corpses, "víctimas de la barbarie roja. . . . Su gobierno, Coronel, anúncielo con cadáveres . . . ¡Corpses! . . . ¡Corpses!" (pp. 108–109)[10]

The grand finale, "Torotumbo," dramatizes the entire fantastic episode as yet another tragic act in the macabre masquerade of a conquered and downtrodden people. But we are left with the hope that the masked *baile* of their years of servitude will one day come to an end, that they will soon discard "el manto de sudor de siglos" and tear off all the deceptive masks of the intruder— "en sus ojos, ya no la sombra de la noche, sino la luz del nuevo dia." (p. 194)[11]

"¡Mejor llamarlas novelas! . . ." because the so-called realities of the moment Asturias wished to record defied all logical treatment. That is why he preferred to report "las cosas que pasan" as seemingly separate and isolated events, as a paradoxical chain of incongruous causes and consequences even though they were in truth but the disparate and diverse fragments of the same historical mosaic of his country's age-old struggle for survival. There is no ordered sequence of events, nor is there any one person or place that stamps the tragedy with a clear sense of unity of purpose and design. And yet there is a pattern in which present and past emerge and commingle to dramatize the eternal enigma of a people caught up in a living past. Is it really too far-fetched to view the Peter Harkins weekend invasion of Guatemala as but a modern version of an older conquest by another people, whose might of yesteryear made the highland rivers run red with the blood of Tecum-Umán and his plumed warriors? Is it too far-fetched, really, to interpret the final episode as the vision of a people who would withdraw from the uneven conflict—leaving behind "todos los disfraces con que se vistió la ciudad para engañarlos"—to reconquer again and yet again the lofty mountains of their retreat, "bajo banderas de plumas azules de quetzal bailando el torotumbo"? (p. 194)[12]

For the hurried analyst, *Week-end en Guatemala* must appear to be an irresponsible and inordinate account. Granted that it defies classification as a novel, that is, a novel in the more formal sense of the term; granted that the individual parts do not clearly constitute a whole; granted that the dissonance of time and timing accentuate the off-beat character of the chronicle; but then might these not be more properly viewed as the very qualities, together with those of language and style, that lend the narrative its epic tone? For Asturias cannot comprehend the current scene as a tightly drawn event of the passing present. It is the need and the will to step beyond the confining limits of "las cosas que pasan" that mark much of his work with the distinctive epic aura of timeless reality. Asturias cannot accept the "eso era antes" with which Alarica Powell dismisses the destructive outbursts of Agua and Fuego as reminders only of a now-dead past; the oppression of those earlier years was still a reality of the present and Milocho's suicidal act of vengeance was testimony to his people's continuing capacity to react in keeping with their ancient cosmic rites.

Asturias is intent on retelling and reinterpreting the intrahistory of his native land, discovering anew the submerged currents that run deep beneath the surface, that surface where the casual observer is aware only of the happenings of the moment (of "las cosas que pasan"). When these deep currents rise on occasion to clash with the visual present, the clash, for Guatemala, is vivid and dramatic— and things are not always what they seem. That is why Asturias turned to the responsive art of fiction where, through the magic power of the word and the imagination, he could create a more enduring and a more revealing image of the contemporary scene. Or rather, a series of scenes, "novelas" or novelettes, that would perforce remind one of tales of horror and the grotesque, of nightmares and dreams and visions and the shattered illusions of men for whom the awful realities of the present appear as the mad creations of their frustrations and fears. "¡Mejor llamarlas novelas! . . ." But truth, they say, is stranger than fiction. This may well be for that fleeting truth momentarily exposed on the naked surface of the present. There is, however, a more incredible truth, a truth so startlingly beyond all credence that nothing short of daringly new techniques would enable the artist to capture it for the receptive and intelligent reader. And it is to this reader that Asturias makes his plea. A less discerning and perceptive mind might toss his creations aside as pure fiction.

Week-end en Guatemala has gone through three editions in Spanish since its first appearance in 1957, and it has been translated into Russian (1958), French (1959), and Italian (1965).[13] Curiously enough, the Havana edition, published by the Imprenta Nacional in 1960, does not carry the epigraph that serves as the burden of these remarks. Probably a printer's oversight! But it does reproduce the author's dedication:

> A GUATEMALA
> mi Patria,
> viva en la sangre
> de sus estudiantes-héroes,
> sus campesinos-mártires,
> sus trabajadores sacrificados
> y su pueblo en lucha.[14]

Week-end en Guatemala is not a great work, and it is not the author's best, but it does ring true in the main to his dual concern for his people and his art. The book was written in haste—and with passion—but not without precedent. Sympathetic to the liberal-leftist leanings of Juan José Arévalo (who, as president from 1944 to 1950 advanced agrarian reform, social security legislation, and restrictive regulation of U.S. firms) and probably impelled to no small degree by the swelling number of social protest novels that won a quick and volatile following during the thirties and the forties, Asturias departed from his early themes, steeped in the folklore and myth of his people, to develop a trilogy in denunciation of the banana trusts and their growing economic, political, and cultural dominance in national life. His so-called "banana trilogy" climaxed the noisy development of a type of fiction that threatened to flourish almost as luxuriantly as the tropical fruit that gave it a unique status in a genre already labelled "la novela anti-imperialista."

The "novela bananera" was a late-bloomer of the species that made its appearance at the turn of the century. It began to emerge in the thirties, its first shoots already sprouting green in the short stories of Carmen Lyra of Costa Rica. During the forties the proliferous plant quickly smothered the older growth beneath its heavy foliage: the Big Stick-Caliban themes of Yankee domination fell to drooping under the friendly warmth of the Good Neighbor sun; while oil and coffee and cane and rubber failed to take deep root anywhere in the area (since they did not present a clear menace to the great masses still living quietly in the confining security of their *tierrecita*). The banana—that same nutritious and bountiful plant that Andrés Bello, in cold and colorless London a century and more ago, had hailed as the first of nature's tropical gifts

> de cuantos concedió bellos presentes
> providencia a las gentes
> del ecuador feliz con mano larga[15]

—had fallen into the hands of unscrupulous adventurers who were greedy for the new species of green gold that threatened to choke off all other national economic growth. The fruit of that all-sustaining plant of Bello's "Oda a la agricultura de la Zona Tórrida"—a plant that "swooned under the weight of its sweet burden"—became unpalatable in the mouths of those who, in fiction, cried out against the monopolies and malpractices of the *fruteras*: of men like Carlos Luis Fallas of Costa Rica in his *Mamita Yunai* (1941), Emilio Quintana of Costa Rica in his *Bananos* (ca. 1941), Joaquín Gutiérrez, also of Costa Rica, in his *Puerto Limón* (1950), and Ramón Amaya-Amador of Honduras in his *Prisión verde* (1950). And in 1950 also Miguel Angel Asturias of Guatemala finally added his uniquely talented voice to the outcry that had swollen to hurricane proportions. Asturias suggestively entitled his first volume *Viento fuerte*,[16] symbolic of the heavy blow, or hurricane, that one day, in the name of human justice, would wreck its sacred vengeance on the despoilers of nature's generous gift to the men of the tropics.[17]

El papa verde,[18] in 1954, and *Los ojos de los enterrados*,[19] in
1960, completed what must be regarded, unquestionably, as
the most ambitious and the best-sustained effort in socio-
economic protest fiction of Latin America to date. The trilogy
does, however, suffer from certain obvious and inevitable
weaknesses. It seems clear that Asturias did not have a well-
developed plan in mind when he started writing *Viento
fuerte*, that he had not yet fully appreciated the epic potential
of his canvas. To move more freely, then, over the expanding
horizon of events and lives and conflicts that demanded more
and more of a role in the story, Asturias was compelled to
bring into play all the tricks and techniques with which he
had experimented in the twenties during his apprenticeship
days in Paris. Perhaps the most challenging of such techniques
are those that compel the reader to be constantly on the alert
for sudden shifts in time sequence and character manipulation. These shifts called for an unusual but necessary repetition and overlap in order to bring past and present into proper
focus for a more rewarding glimpse into the future. To attempt to retell the story step by step from volume to volume
would be disastrous. Had Asturias structured his narrative in
straight-line fashion, it would still have been a good story but
it would have lost much, if not all, of its epic sweep and much
of the ebb and flow of situation and circumstance that illumine the darker side of the evolving scene. For the more
immediate purpose of these remarks, then, it will be more ap-
propriate to summarize the essential argument of the three
volumes as one.

Against a broad backdrop of fictional characters and happenings that in almost every instance evoke their easily recog-
nizable counterparts in the true chronicle of the banana empire in Guatemala, Asturias develops his story—and his case—
in the light of the legend of those one-time colorful Yankee
adventurers who gambled on the potential wealth to be won

in the large-scale cultivation of the lowly banana. It is the story of their unscrupulous and often ruthless struggle for power and of their chameleonic rise from the romantic role of petty pirates in the Caribbean to a place among the economic barons of copper and meat and railroads and chewing gum. The chronicle of their success is dramatized in the living legend of one of the author's strongest characters, Geo Maker Thompson, who, when but still a young freebooter hailed as "el Papa de la piratería," already aspired to be known one day as "el Papa Verde"—Banana's King. Those pioneer soldiers-of-fortune were of the heroic breed who came to battle in the epic spirit of conquest: to build bridges and railroads and routes in the sky, to mine, to filibuster, to plunder, and, yes, even to carve "empires (economic empires) in the wilderness." They did come to plunder, but they also came to stay and to build—build for themselves and for those with whom they had cast their lot. This pioneer spirit, however, had long been lost, and in the wake of the Maker Thompsons came the faceless subordinates who continue the exploitation, directed now by big-moneyed interests from the U.S.A. An enlightened American, one of those pioneers who remained to regret the day when it could be said that "sin riesgo no hay aventura vital" (and they are not wanting in Asturias), remarked emphatically on the change: "¡Hubo, porque la hubo, la hora de la epopeya; pero ahora, qué quieren ustedes, es una vulgar explotación, una torpe explotación de recursos naturales, de tierras inestimables que nosotros despreciamos!"[20]

This torpid exploitation by foreign-based interests has also had its strong opposition from within the monopoly itself. There is, for example, the mysterious and popular Cosi of *Viento fuerte* ("aquel chiflado inofensivo" to his fellow-gringos in the tropics), who began as a travelling salesman of "todo lo indispensable para el costurero" to become as Lester Stoner, alias Lester Mead, one of the millionaire stockholders

of the Tropical Platanera, S.A. *Viento fuerte* is the story of his
fight to restore vitality to the tired venture and to cleanse it of
its accumulated sores of immoral and inhuman practices. Asturias focuses his charges through Lester's eyes and those of
his wife Leland, who had rebelled against the boredom of
being like most Americans in the tropics: "ni buenos ni malos,
ni alegres ni tristes, simplemente máquinas." (p. 29) Lester
carries his fight to Chicago, to the very presence of the "Green
Pope" himself:

> . . . un señor que está metido en una oficina y tiene a sus
> órdenes millones de dólares. Mueve un dedo y camina o se
> detiene un barco. Dice una palabra y se compra una República.
> Estornuda y se cae un Presidente, General o Licenciado. . . .
> Frota el trasero en la silla y estalla una revolución. Contra ese
> señor tenemos que luchar. (p. 99)[21]

Lester's fight takes the form of setting up a new company,
with Guatemalan associates, to break down the stifling monopoly of the "Tropicaltanera," so nicknamed by the natives
because of its high-handed attitudes and practices. The good
fight of the high-minded Americans Lester and Leland constitutes the central theme of *Viento fuerte*. Lester and Leland
were not destined to see good win over evil, for they too were
to die as victims of the hurricane, or "viento fuerte," the storm
of protest and retribution, the only force that someday would
be strong enough to sweep away the evil and the injustices
of anonymous moneyed power. Lester and Leland had a pre-
monition that such a day would come to pass:

> . . . Por unos puñados de dinero, por el dominio de estas plan-
> taciones, por las riquezas que aun fragmentadas en dividendos
> anuales, son millones y millones de dólares, perdimos el mundo,
> no la dominación del mundo, ésa la tenemos, sino la posesión
> del mundo, que es diferente; ahora somos dueños de todas estas
> tierras, de estas tentaciones verdes, somos señores; pero no

debemos olvidar que el tiempo del demonio es limitado y que llegará la hora de Dios, que es la hora del hombre. . . . La hora del hombre será el "viento fuerte" que de abajo de las entrañas de la tierra alce su voz de reclamo, y exija, y barra con todos nosotros. . . . (pp. 117–118)[22]

Lester and Leland were sacrificed, but their struggle was not in vain, because the courage and money and lands they passed on to their Guatemalan colleagues made it possible for the seedling of national interest to survive and grow strong.

El papa verde is the chronicle of Maker Thompson's rise from "navegador en el Caribe" to "navegador en el sudor humano" and, ultimately, to absolute power as the head of a new American state. This new state came to be known as "la República Frutera . . . más fuerte que cualquiera de las otras Repúblicas de intereses limitados o canaleros . . . ," a state that proudly unfurled its own flag, "la no menos gloriosa de nuestro Estado Frutero, consistente en un paño verde, y al centro una calavera corsaria sobre dos ramas de bananal."[23] The novel ends with the settlement of a boundary dispute between Honduras and Guatemala, a settlement that results much more importantly in a definitive victory for Maker Thompson, who emerges from the confrontation as the president of the most powerful fruit consortium in the world or, as Asturias puns with his usual easy irony, "¡Un emporio! ¡Un emporio de civilización y de progreso . . . Emporialistas en lugar de imperialistas!" (p. 264) But the steadily closing jaws of economic imperialism are of no concern to the masses who celebrate the empty national victory in their traditional way: "¡Qué importa . . . si hay feriado . . . Júbilo. Júbilo rodando. Júbilo andando . . . Bailes en las plazas. *Te Deum* en la Catedral!" (p. 653)[24] Nevertheless, Asturias does drop a hint here and there that resistance and rebellion are in the offing. In contrast to a total absence of pride in their own land and to an infectious greed easily acquired from the gringo that

prompted the heirs of Lester Mead to sell out to the *frutera*,
the novel offers us the first signs of protest from the disin-
herited, who cry for their just share of the lands promised
them under an agrarian reform that falters and fails: "Repártanlas . . . , repartan las tierras. . . . Repártanlas . . . repártanlas . . . repártanlas." And the cry was to echo and reecho
"hasta que llegue el día de la venganza que verán los ojos de
los enterrados, más numerosos que las estrellas, y se beba la jí-
cara con sangre." (p. 303)[25]

Los ojos de los enterrados is the answer to the people's cry.
It is the final episode in the epic emergence and dominance
of an evil power inimical to national integrity and to ele-
mental human justice. It is the story of another gathering
storm, one, this time, that will not destroy the plantation but
rather bring with it a new will to resist, a growing sense of
national unity, an effective political appeal, "la de las masas
revolucionarias," through a nation-wide general strike before
which both "el Señor Presidente" and "el Papa Verde" will
fall together ("y ya podían cerrar los ojos los enterrados que
esperaban el día de la justicia").[26] Like all imaginative literature the novels of this trilogy of social protest are fiction, not
fact, and any resemblance to persons or events is, presumably,
pure happenstance. But Asturias plies his art with such con-
summate skill, never openly revealing his presence or position, that the reader is easily drawn into the illusion that the
raw materials of historical truth do, indeed, read like fiction,
like a good *roman à clef*. Furthermore, the novels are replete
with all the ingredients that constitute, as we would be given
to understand, the human drama of economic and cultural
conflict in the tropics: the aimless, amoral existence of the
average American without roots and without character, eternally bathed in whiskey and sweat; the contrast between the
American's hygienic isolation behind screened doors and win-
dows and the ageless universe outside, a world of maize and

beans, of bird and myth, of jungle and legend ("fuera el rugido, dentro el fonógrafo; fuera el paisaje, dentro la fotografía; fuera las esencias embriagantes, dentro las botellas de whiskeys"), the denial of ancient customs and beliefs and even names in a futile effort to take on the protective coloring of an alien culture (". . . ir buscando nombres de gente bien, porque los nuestros eran puros rascuaches y de pobres y eso por no ofendernos, pues más parecen de irracionales. Arsenia de nombre perra y Gaudelia nombre de yegua . . ."—and the venerable name of Cojubul takes on the foreign tone of Keijebul);[27] and, finally, there are the countless scenes and episodes and manners and legends that give full body to the skeletal account of an epic struggle between good and evil.

Content, however, is not enough. Even in writings solidly based on fact the key to masterful presentation is verbal skill. There is, happily, sharply mounting testimony to the fact that even historical and socio-economic treatises need not necessarily be wastelands of gawky form and lusterless prose. In its premodernist garb Latin American fiction was largely a tasteless document of manners and polemics. However, since the turn of the century and especially in the past twenty-five years, the novel and the short story have attained a position of indisputable competitive strength. The number of candidates for Western World awards in all forms crowds the roster of the deserving. Bandeira of Brazil, Borges of Argentina, Gallegos of Venezuela, Neruda of Chile are still among the recent living contenders for the most prestigious prize of all. In 1945 the Nobel Prize was awarded to a Latin American writer for the first time. The beloved Chilean poetess Gabriela Mistral (1889–1957) won that first award. And in 1967, after years of heavy contention for another Latin American winner, the coveted prize fell to Miguel Angel Asturias. Ordinarily the award is made for an author's latest achievement, without specifying any particular work. A recent trend appears to favor writers "more for their political inclinations than for their literary work."[28] And the Nobel citation does refer specifically to *Viento fuerte* as an account of the "battle against domination by the North American trust in the form of the United Fruit Company and its political economic consequences in the present day history of the banana republic."[29] Most unfortunately, the choice of the novel and the thoroughly infelicitous phrasing of the commendation lend full credence to the charge. But it is not our intention to argue over matters of literary taste and misguided emphasis. There may be more justification for the forthright statement of the Soviet Lenin Peace Prize committee when, in 1966, they honored Asturias for his works that "expose American intervention against the Guatemalan people."[30] Nevertheless, we cannot refrain from stating our preference for *Los ojos de los enterrados* as the best of the four works that would appear to have carried most weight in the deliberations of the Swedish Academy. And again availing ourselves of the privilege of dissent, we can only express regret that Asturias should have been honored largely, if not exclusively, for a body of writing that testifies only in part to the enduring qualities of his literary talent. We would not deny that the author has made a signal contribution to "protest" literature. Rather we would insist that in assessing the works in question we should bear in mind the author's own words of caution—"¡Mejor llamarlas novelas! ..."[1]—and judge them less for the "things" they would reveal and more for the artistic skill with which he adds yet another dimension to a reality that can only be understood in terms of the absurd. Latter-day critics have labelled this new dimension as "magical realism."[31]

Artistic skill is, fortunately, still satisfyingly palpable in these protest novels by Asturias. For some, certain linguistic and stylistic techniques and mannerisms may seem out of place in the context of the "things" that transpire in the narrative. But on the whole the author has achieved a happy amalgam of theme, tone, and technique, and it is precisely in this that his message and manner are superior to all other similarly sustained efforts in Latin American literature. Even in his novels of protest Asturias is always fully alert to the potentially effective factors of language and style. And just as he is cautious to a remarkable degree in holding back from direct ideological intrusion in the thesis, to a like degree he is commendably successful in holding language and style to their proper role as discreet handmaidens to the story.

However fragmented the several excerpts cited herein may be, it must be clear that Asturias is intrigued by the magic power of the word, that he gives the word full rein as an entity of endless subtle and suggestive meaning and as an instrument of infinite creative potential. It is equally clear that his mastery of an enviable variety of techniques is the product of a long apprenticeship in the manipulation of spontaneous and proverbial utterance, of image and symbol, of ingenious word play, of richly variegated phrasing, of repetition and reiteration and enumeration, of parallelisms and disjunctive contrasts, of onomatopoeia, of distortion, of the grotesque and absurd, of fiction and fact, of horror and of fear, of folklore and legend and myth. Even the four protest novels would provide a generous sampling of the author's master craftsmanship. But as a linguist and stylist Asturias is at his best when theme and mood and tempo demand an all-out effort in his attempt to illumine the Guatemalan mystique and to reconstruct the epic of the Maya where land and man and animal, past and present, converge in cosmic unity.

To recount the significant facts of the life story of Guatemala's honored writer and to analyze the elements of his fictional art would require far more time than this occasion allows.[32] For to do it well, the story must begin in 1899 in Guatemala City, where Miguel Angel Asturias was born of a

Spanish father and an Indian mother. It must tell of how as a
youth he came to know the Indian way of life and of how he
intervened actively in 1920 in the overthrow of the dictator
Manuel Estrada Cabrera, adding that he was not a stranger
to the irritant of the student strike, to the maddening darkness of the political jail—nor yet to his country's endemic
submission to seismal scourge. The story would continue with
the youth's abandonment of medicine and his earning of a
degree in law in 1922 upon the completion of his dissertation
on "El problema social del indio."

A number of seeds had taken deep root with birth and during those early student days in his homeland: one, a quicken-
ing concern for the Indian, whose blood ran full and firm in
his physical and spiritual makeup; the other, a compulsive
urge to share in any demand for political and social change.
These concerns and these compulsions were to flower during
the years he would spend in Paris between 1923 and 1933. For
three years he studied the culture and the religion of the Maya
with Georges Raynaud of the Sorbonne. His dedication bore
early fruit: with J.M. Hurtado de Mendoza he translated
Raynaud's version of the *Popol-Vuh* and the *Anales de los
xahil*; he composed his *Leyendas de Guatemala*; and finally,
and more importantly for literature, because of his compelling
interest in the theories and manner of the cubists and sur-
realists, he came to see his country in startlingly new perspective: ". . . todo, hombres, paisajes, cosas, flota en un clima
surrealista, de locura de imágenes yuxtapuestas."[33] The formula was at hand, and in the elaboration of an effective technique Asturias turned also to draw heavily on the poetic sym-
bolism of the language and the myth of the Maya as revealed
in the *Popol-Vuh*. For his experimentation with the element
of dreams and with automatic writing and his abandoning
pure fantasy in search of concrete associations ("mediante
la simple evocación de los sonidos") heightened his apprecia-

tion for and his understanding of the Mayan concept of poetry and the spoken word: ". . . el apareamiento o la yuxtaposición de palabras que, como dicen los indios, nunca se han encontrado antes. Porque así es como el indio define la poesía. Dice que la poesía es donde las palabras se encuentran por primera vez."[34]

Leyendas de Guatemala, his first book, was five years (1925–1930) in the making. Asturias dedicated the legends to his mother: "A mi madre que me contaba cuentos." Memory of childhood tales, tradition enriched through rewarding research in the sacred books of his people, style forged out of the poetic ritual and myth of the Maya and the most advanced of modern literary experimentation, here are the elements that have given an original stamp to these tales of "mannered translation" and poetic prose, even much more so to *El Señor Presidente* and *Hombres de maíz*, that were to follow. And Guatemala in her ancient beliefs and customs and in her modern trauma would become the central concern of his art.

El Señor Presidente, his second book, would also be long in gestation. Although a first draft had been signed in Guatemala in December of 1922, and reworkings had been completed in Paris in 1925 and again in 1932, the novel did not appear until 1946. And though obviously not aimed at dictator Jorge Ubico (1930–1944), the devastating indictment was more than any self-respecting censorship could condone. Clearly the setting is Guatemala and clearly "el Señor Presidente" is none other than Manuel Estrada Cabrera, whom Asturias had helped overthrow. But the author does not say so, for it was not his intention to place the story in finite time and space. And yet Asturias has recorded the Estrada era artistically for all time. The reality he creates is one in which little men move fitfully about in a Dantesque world of darkness and terror and cruelty and horror, of opportunism and servility, scurrying vainly from a pernicious presence that permeates every physical, spiritual, and moral fiber of their being. The presence is more terrifying than that of a dictator; it is more pervasive even than that of dictatorship; it is, in fact, the very personification of the most dreadful experience known to man; it is nothing less than Fear itself. The theme is of universal import and the treatment is on a par with that of a small company of magicians who have succeeded in recasting reality on a higher plane and in a full-dimensional mold. Technically, too, *El Señor Presidente* is a thoroughly exciting book. It has been analyzed fully a number of times.[35] At this point we can only add that the total experience of theme, treatment, and effect will not prove disappointing—not even in translation.[36]

Hombres de maíz is the full fruit of the author's total absorption in the mythological legacy of the Maya as revealed in the *Popol-Vuh* and in the role of the folk in the socioeconomic development of modern Guatemala.[37] *Hombres de maíz* is a complex book, one difficult to classify and one open to a wide range of contradictory interpretations. A novel, a symphonic poem, a popular epic, a model of stylistic virtuosity, a fine amalgam of myth and reality. The author may have been too humble and too modest (but also perhaps more accurate) when he stated that the basic theme of the book is rooted in the conflict between the sons of the ancient Maya ("of yellow corn and of white corn they made their flesh") and the *ladinos* or *criollos* of later days when the lessons of the *Popol-Vuh* no longer held any meaning: ". . . se inspira en la lucha sostenida entre el indígena del campo que entiende que el maíz debe sembrarse sólo para alimento y el hombre criollo que lo siembra para negocio, quemando bosques de maderas preciosas y empobreciendo la tierra para enriquecerse."[38]

Then, in that same year of 1949, Asturias shifts his emphasis to another phase of his country's epic struggle for survival. The struggle now is one that will decide whether the children of maize and the sons of Alvarado, in common combat against a common foe, can achieve and maintain national identity and a modern socio-economic way of life consonant with their age-old customs and beliefs. The "banana cycle" and *Week-end en Guatemala* are an account of that struggle.

What follows cannot be told here; of the author's years in the diplomatic and cultural service of his country (he is presently ambassador to France), of his work as a dramatist and a poet, of his more recent prose writings (especially of *Mulata de tal*, published in 1963, which in late 1967 became the third of his novels to be translated into English), of his growing popularity in other lands and tongues.[39] But our text has imposed certain limitations that chronometric time would guard with something akin to Mayan reverence for the sacred word of their beginnings. We must bow, therefore, before the modern tyranny of that old deity Cronus, but before we do, one final word.

> ¿No ve las cosas que pasan? . . .
> ¡Mejor llamarlas novelas! . . .

The Asturias of our text has given us a portrait of Guatemala that only a master of the written word could have recreated out of legend and fact on the incredible canvas of an account of the "things" that have come to pass down through the years since that first account in the *Popol-Vuh* of "how all was in suspense, all calm, in silence; all motionless, still, and the expanse of the sky was empty. . . . Only by a miracle, only by magic art . . . was the earth created . . . and they made perfect the work, when they did it after thinking and meditating upon it.[40] Asturias has dedicated his magic art toward a more perfect understanding of that miracle of reality we know as Guatemala.

Notes

[1] "Don't you see the things that are happening? . . . T'would be better to call them novels! . . ." —Miguel Angel Asturias, *Week-end en Guatemala*

(Buenos Aires, 1957). [The editor is responsible for the English translations in the notes.]

[2] "Living a dream without dreams . . ." —Asturias, *Week-end en Guatemala* (La Habana, 1960), p. 15. Succeeding references will be to this edition and will be incorporated in the text proper.

[3] "Only while drunk could I believe that my country, the most powerful country in the world, could be at war with a country so small, so inoffensive . . . ha . . . ha . . . ha! . . . it was a shame, and it was necessary to be totally, absolutely, completely drunk, and to continue that way, to believe it . . . drunk . . . dead drunk. . . ."

[4] "the cruelties of those who decimated the indigenous population, hanged their chieftains, crushed their people. . . ."

[5] "blonde swallow" . . . "That belongs to the past, darling, that belongs to the past; nowadays volcanos are like you. . . . They are good for nothing!"

[6] ". . . Ocelotle 33 has gone away . . . it was a nightmare, and you wake up from nightmares. . . ." "You wake up from a nightmare, but not from reality. No one can wake up from reality."

[7] "that which your father proclaimed . . . to have children for the state."

[8] "Yes, a dream which as fire set in a clearing quickly goes out!" . . . "masters of our misery, of our ruin, of our poverty. . . ." —It was a dream, Nana Caida! / —Yes, a dream. . . .

[9] "One hundred sixty million gringos, young and old . . . ha! . . . ha! the most powerful company in all the Caribbean . . . ha! . . . ha! . . . the Catholic church of New York, of the country, and of the whole world . . . ha! . . . ha! . . . three Presidents of three Republics, at least, ha! . . . ha! . . . chains of newspapers and news agencies . . . ha! . . . ha! . . . the latest automatic weapons . . . ha! . . . ha! . . . showers of dollars, bombers, high ranking military leaders ready to surrender when they see the tide turn in our favor . . . and an army of mercenaries . . . ha! . . . ha! . . . Tiburcio Sotoj . . . Guadalupe Sotoj . . . Rufino Sotoj . . . ha! . . . ha! . . . against so rich a menu as that what could you agrarians possibly do . . . ha! . . . ha . . . ha . . . ha! . . ."

[10] "Better in English than in Spanish. . . . In English the word had an unusual sound like that of the peck or cry of a bird of prey" . . . "victims of the red hoarde. . . . See that your government announces it, Colonel, with bodies, dead bodies . . . ."

[11] "the centuries-old cloak of sweat" . . . "in their eyes, no longer the shadow of night, but the light of the new day."

[12] . . . "all the disguises which the city wore in order to deceive them" . . . "under the banners of the blue quetzal plumes, dancing the *torotumbo*?"

[13] The third Spanish edition is that of the *Obras escogidas*, 3 vols. (Madrid, 1955–1961). There is still no English translation. Also, Aguilar has published *Obras completas*, Biblioteca Premios Nobel, 3 vols. (Madrid, 1968).

[14] "TO GUATEMALA / my Country, / may she live in the blood / of her student-heroes, / her rural martyrs, / her sacrificial workers, / and her people in strife."

[15] "of all the beautiful gifts that Providence did bestow with a gener-

ous hand on the peoples of the happy tropics." See Englekirk *et al.*, *An Anthology of Spanish American Literature*, 2nd ed. (New York, 1968), Vol. I, p. 120, lines 53–55.

16 Miguel Angel Asturias, *Viento fuerte* (Guatemala, 1949) and (Buenos Aires, 1950). There are also translations into French (1955), Slavic (1958), Italian (1965), and English (1967). The first English translation (London, 1967) is by Darwin Flakoll and Claribell Alegría. The latest English translation (New York, 1969) is by Gregory Rabassa.

17 For two studies that deal with anti-imperialism in general and with banana interests in particular in Middle American prose fiction, see Miriam H. Thompson, *Anti-Imperialism as Reflected in the Prose Fiction of Middle America* (Doctoral dissertation, Tulane University, 1955); Eneida Avila, *Las compañías bananeras en la novelística centroamericana* (Doctoral dissertation, Tulane University, 1959).

18 Miguel Angel Asturias, *El papa verde* (Buenos Aires, 1954). There are also translations into French (1955–1959) and Italian (1959).

19 Miguel Angel Asturias, *Los ojos de los enterrados* (Buenos Aires, 1960).

20 There was, indeed, a period of epic adventure but now, what else can we expect but a vulgar exploitation, a stupid exploitation of natural resources, of lands which we ourselves scorned!" Asturias, *Viento fuerte*, (Buenos Aires, 1955), pp. 30–31. Succeeding references will be to this edition and will be incorporated in the text proper.

21 . . . "neither good nor bad, neither happy nor sad, simply machines." . . . ". . . a lord who reigns from an office and has millions of dollars at his disposal. He moves a finger and starts or stops a ship. He speaks and a Republic is bought. He sneezes and a President, General, or Attorney falls. . . . He twists in his chair and a revolution breaks out. That is the man we have to fight against."

22 "Because of a paltry sum of money, the control of these plantations, and the wealth which even in annual dividends amounts to millions and millions of dollars, we lost the world; not the domination of the world, we have that, but the possession of the world, which is different. Now we are the masters of all these lands, we are the proprietors of this green temptation; but we should not forget that the devil's time is limited and that God's hour, which is man's hour, is sure to arrive. . . . Man's hour will be the hurricane which from below, from the bowels of the earth, will raise its clamoring voice, and make demands, and sweep us all away. . . ."

23 ". . . the Fruit Republic . . . stronger than any of the other Republics of limited business affairs or canal zone interests" . . . "the no less glorious one of our Fruit State, consisting of a green background, and in the center a pirate skull over two branches of a banana plant."—Miguel Angel Asturias, *El papa verde*, in *Obras escogidas*, Vol. 2, p. 404. Further references will be to this edition and will be incorporated in the text proper.

24 "An emporium! An emporium of civilization and progress . . . Emporialists instead of imperialists!" . . . "What does it matter . . . if there is a holiday . . . Jubilation. Joyous jubilation. Jubilant jubilation . . . Dancing in the plazas. *Te Deum* in the Cathedral!"

[25] "Divide it . . . , divide the land . . . Divide it . . . divide it . . . divide it." . . . "until the coming of the day of vengeance, the day when the eyes of the interred, more numerous than the stars, will see again, and the cup of blood will be tasted."

[26] "and then the dead who were awaiting the day of justice would be able to sleep."—Asturias, *El papa verde*, p. 482.

[27] ". . . to seek names of the upper classes, because ours were mere trivia and of the lowly; and we put it in these terms so as not to cause ourselves undue offense, for, in truth, our names were more like those of animals. Arsenia, the name of a bitch; and Gaudelia, the name of a mare . . ."—Asturias, *El papa verde*, p. 49.

[28] *Britannica Book of the Year*, 1968, p. 138.

[29] *Britannica Book of the Year*, 1968, p. 138.

[30] *Britannica Book of the Year*, 1968, p. 138.

[31] For reactions to the 1967 award, see Alexander Coleman, "Why Asturias?" *The New York Times Book Review*, November 19, 1967, pp. 1–2 and 89; Thomas E. Lyon, "Miguel Angel Asturias: Timeless Fantasy. The 1967 Nobel Prize for Literature," *Books Abroad*, Vol. 42 (Spring, 1968), pp. 183–189; and Robert G. Mead, Jr., "Miguel Angel Asturias and the Nobel Prize," *Hispania*, Vol. 51 (1968), pp. 326–331. For a history of the origin and development of the Nobel awards, see H. Schück, R. Sohlman, *et al.*, *Nobel. The Man and his Prizes* (Amsterdam, London, and New York, 1962). And for an assessment of prizes already awarded and of neglected literary areas both of fruition and promise, see "Nobel Prize Symposium," *Books Abroad*, Vol. 41 (Winter, 1967), pp. 5–45.

[32] From among a growing number of more general studies on the man and his work, see especially: Seymour Menton, "Miguel Angel Asturias: realidad y fantasía," in his *Historia crítica de la novela guatemalteca* (Guatemala, 1960), pp. 195–241; Atilio Jorge Castelpoggi, *Miguel Angel Asturias* (Buenos Aires, 1961); Fernando Alegría, "Miguel Angel Asturias, novelista del viejo y del nuevo mundo," *Memoria del Octavo Congreso del Instituto Internacional de Literatura Iberoamericana* (México, 1961), pp. 131–141; see also his *Historia de la novela hispanoamericana*, 3rd ed. (México, 1966), pp. 221–225; José Antonio Galaos, "Los dos ejes de la novelística de Miguel Angel Asturias," *Cuadernos hispanoamericanos*, Vol. 52 (October, 1962), pp. 126–139; Francis Donahue, "M. A. Asturias—Protest in the Guatemalan Novel," *Discourse*, Vol. 10 (1967), pp. 83–96; Luis Harss and Barbara Dohmann, "Miguel Angel Asturias," *Into the Mainstream. Conversations with Latin American Writers* (New York, 1967), pp. 68–101; Carlos Rincón, "M. A. Asturias," *Eco*, Vol. 15 (1967), pp. 565–588.

[33] ". . . everything—men, landscapes, things—floats in a surrealistic climate of madness of juxtaposed images."—Quoted by Rincón, "M. A. Asturias," *Eco*, pp. 565–588, from Rómulo Gallegos on *El papa verde* in *Síntesis*, Vol. 4 (San Salvador, July, 1954), p. 25.

[34] ". . . the pairing or the juxtaposition of words which, as the Indians say, have never before been used together. Because this is how the Indian defines poetry. He says that poetry is where words meet for the first time."— Rincón, "M. A. Asturias," *Eco*, pp. 565–588.

35 See Note 32 above. For several additional studies that deal specifically with the novel, see Richard L. Franklin, "Observations on *El Señor Presidente*," *Hispania*, Vol. 44 (1967), pp. 683–685; Richard J. Callan, "Babylonian Mythology in *El Señor Presidente*," *Hispania*, Vol. 50 (1967), pp. 417–424.

36 The first printing (1963) of the English translation by Frances Partridge bore the title *The President*; the third printing (1967) carries the title of the original Spanish, *El Señor Presidente*, a seemingly insignificant detail, but it is details such as these that shorten one mite more the illusory bridge between an original and its deceptive counterpart in translation.

37 Miguel Angel Asturias, *Hombres de maíz* (Buenos Aires, 1949).

38 ". . . is inspired in the struggle sustained between the Indian of the fields who understands that corn ought to be sown only for food, and the Creole who plants it for business, burning forests of precious woods and impoverishing the land in order to enrich himself."—"Homenaje a Miguel Angel Asturias," *Repertorio americano*, Vol. 44 (March 1, 1950), p. 83.

39 Miguel Angel Asturias, *Mulata de tal* (Buenos Aires, 1963). The English translation, *Mulata*, was "admirably" done by Gregory Rabassa for the Delacorte Press, New York. For a summary of the novel and a preview of the translation, see Robert G. Mead, Jr., in the *Saturday Review*, November 4, 1967, p. 32.

40 *Popol-Vuh*, trans. by Delia Goetz and Sylvanus G. Morley from the Spanish version of Adrián Recinos (Norman, Oklahoma, 1950), pp. 81, 83–84.

John Vogt, Jr.

Euclides da Cunha: Spokesman of the New Brazilian Nationalism

Brazilians moved into the twentieth century on a wave of great optimism for the future of their nation. Despite economic setbacks in the 1890's, all indicators of national life now showed a Brazil that was moving rapidly forward. Coffee prices on the world market had been stabilized, its production in Brazil was good,[1] and the rubber industry was creating a boom in the Amazon Basin.[2] The military revolts of the last decade of the nineteenth century seemed far removed from this new Brazilian era of progress. A national census in 1900 revealed that the nation had nearly doubled its population in little more than a quarter of a century.[3] New immigrants were actively engaged in pushing Brazil's frontiers of settlement westward beyond the old colonial limits of the country and into virgin lands. (This idea of peopling the land and opening the interior has been very important in twentieth-century Brazil.) The administrations of Presidents Rodrigues Alves (1902–6) and Afonso Pena (1906–9) gave strong support to the westward movement.[4] The network of national railways began to inch out into the valleys and plateaus west of the São Francisco River.[5] Colonel Rondón and his engineers were busy linking the hinterland with the coastal cities by telegraph.[6] The diplomatic successes of the Baron of Rio Branco in rounding out Brazil's territorial claims,[7] and the activities abroad of the noted jurist Rui Barbosa served to heighten the people's pride in their nation and their belief in the unlimited possibilities before them. In the midst of this activity, preparations were being made for a national exposition in Rio in 1908, to commemorate the arrival of the Portuguese Crown in Brazil a century before.

Concurrent with the economic and expansionist activities, intellectual leaders of this new Brazil were taking stock of the general condition of the country after the first chaotic decade of the Republic. Among the subjects being scrutinized was the perplexing issue of the Canudos War. By 1900 the passions of the rebellion in the backlands of the State of Bahia had subsided. It was easier now for Brazilians to discern the errors of this conflict, viewed at the proper distance and in perspective.

During the rebellion itself, the civil disorder and division that plagued the country had caused public opinion to lash out against the supposed monarchist revolt directed by the rebels. The Brazilian citizen living in Rio, São Paulo, or Bahia could not understand the motives of Antônio Maciel and his devotees in the backlands, with their belief in a resurrected King Sebastian and their antirepublican views.[8] Clearly, a show of force in this region by government military forces was deemed essential if the rebels were to be contained. But defeats of government troops had followed one another in rapid succession, and the papers, reporting early sketchy dispatches from the front, blew up the affair out of proportion. Finally, after a year of bloody combat, on October 5, 1897, the battlefield fell silent. To suppress the rebels the federal government had sent more than thirteen thousand troops into the field and had resorted to frightful massacres. Instead of being captured, the fanatical supporters of Maciel had chosen to fight to the death. All but a handful of ragged, starving women and children perished in the combat and the fire that swept over the town of Canudos, following its capture.[9] There was no celebration by the victorious army that had hammered down upon Canudos in this struggle. Instead, the basic weakness of the Republic's military had been made painfully evident.

The Canudos War had failed to provide a permanent solution to the problems of the economically depressed Northeast. But the young republic survived, and soon the memory of the war grew dimmer. Then, in 1902, Euclides da Cunha, who had accompanied the republican army into the *sertão* six years before as a young newspaper reporter, brought the battles of the war squarely before the Brazilian public once more. Da Cunha's book, *Os Sertões*, born out of the author's experience in this tragedy in the backlands, was destined to become Brazil's first great work of social protest.[10]

Euclides da Cunha belongs to that elite group of Brazilian scholars who, after the fall of the Empire, continued to question the philosophical path their nation was pursuing. For da Cunha, *Os Sertões* was more than simply a narrative of the gruesome events at Canudos; it was his challenge to the conscience of the nation for her actions there. It stimulated similar endeavors by other authors to examine their own land, particularly that vast portion of the nation removed from the urban centers of population along the eastern seaboard. The literary works of men like da Cunha and his contemporary Graça Aranha enlightened Brazilians about an area of their country of which most urban dwellers had very little knowledge. It also introduced the urban population to a new element in the Brazilian social structure. This was the *sertanejo*, or backlander, who inhabited the often hostile land of the *sertão* in the Brazilian interior.

One of the main criticisms leveled upon Brazilian society by da Cunha's *Os Sertões* was that, during the first decade of republican life, Brazil had been unable to emancipate herself from dominant European philosophical trends and European intellectual mentors. In the program of expansion undertaken by the military regimes of Deodoro da Fonseca and Floriano Peixoto, Brazil's leaders were following a path laid down by contemporary European nations, such as England and Germany, in their own expansionist policies. Brazilian military and governmental leaders, schooled in European tactics of warfare and diplomacy, looked to the imperial campaigns of these nations as models for their own frontier expansion. National spirit was high. The Republic was established, but social forces capable of toppling the new government still existed within the country. And any opposing forces, like the religious fanatics gathering at Canudos in 1895, were felt to threaten the security of the state. Therefore, the proved Bismarckian tactics of "Blood and Iron" seemed warranted for colonizing the frontier against the opposition of the *sertanejo*.[11] These rebels could not be allowed to disregard government orders for fear that other groups of malcontents or monarchists would join them or follow their lead.

What da Cunha portrays in the cultural life of Brazil in this period is a "second-hand civilization."[12] Brazilians had adopted many of the outward manifestations of European civilization and thought without fully comprehending the underlying principles.[13] On their new national banner they had emblazoned the positivist principle of "Order and Progress." Yet in their republican revolutionary zeal, the radical Jacobins in the cities and the government only widened the gulf between the life of the Brazilian cities and the primitive society of Brazil's native sons of the *sertão*. So wide had the breach grown that by 1896 and the Canudos rebellion, the *sertanejos* were more alien to Brazilian urban society than were the immigrants fresh off the boats from Europe. As da Cunha himself states: "It was not an ocean that separated us from them, but three whole centuries."[14] No one in Brazil at that time could conceive of these ragged backlanders as being capable of throwing back expedition after expedition of government troops with terrible losses. The only logical explanation seemed to be that the rebellion heralded an attempt by the dispossessed monarchists to regain power. A mass meeting of the citizenry of Rio in March, 1896, voiced its belief that the rebels at Canudos indeed were monarchist "gangsters," and the Cariocans pledged their active support to the government in suppressing the revolt.[15]

So da Cunha recalled the Canudos campaign to the public, but he was not concerned with fictitious monarchical plots or military incompetency. Although filled with geological and topographical allusions, Os Sertões in 1902 was the first attempt to redefine the bases of Brazilian nationalism and to recognize the backlanders as forming a significant part of the Brazilian nation.

Before reviewing da Cunha's position regarding Brazilian nationalism, let us examine briefly just what is meant by nationalism as it affected Brazil. Since the eighteenth century, definitions of the word "nationalism" have multiplied, so that today it carries a number of connotations. In addition to chauvinism, it means national spirit, national consciousness, national thought, and even national policy. In the writing of history the word has generally been used since the 1920's to denote a theory as well. Hence, the term "age of nationalism."[16] Thus the term is capable of evoking conflicting images, depending upon the context in which it is used. This does not mean that simpler, broader definitions of "nationalism" have not been attempted. The noted political scientist Hans Kohn, while writing on nationalism in the 1920's, defined the concept as "a state of mind, in which the supreme loyalty of the individual is felt to be due to the nation state."[17] This definition, though acceptable as far as it goes, still does not enable the scholar to apply it to particular circumstances. A more useful approach to defining the term, used by many political scientists, is to divide nationalism into types, according to the most important meaning of the word for themselves and the particular set of conditions they are seeking to describe. Among historians, Carlton J. H. Hayes divides modern nationalism into five major categories.[18] The Brazilian manifestation of nationalism in the 1890's seems best to fit one of the classifications laid down by Hayes: integral nationalism. As Hayes defines it, integral nationalism inherited the national and historical traditions of nationalism. However, it made the nation not a means to humanity but an end in itself. The spirit of integral nationalism was hostile to internationalism; it was jingoistic, militant, and inclined to imperialism. In domestic affairs integral nationalism was highly illiberal and sought to oblige all citizens to conform to a common standard of manners and morals. It subordinated all personal liberties to its own purpose. All this it would do "in the national interest." Hayes indicates that Auguste Comte and his positivist philosophy were major forerunners of integral nationalism.[19]

Euclides da Cunha voices similar conclusions in *Os Sertões* when speaking of public opinion in the early years of the Republic. He speaks of individuals who were devoid of any ideas or objectives, and who confined their thinking to preserving the new republic at any cost. Their exaggerated enthusiasm for Jacobinism made possible all sorts of excesses, one of which came to be the bloody Canudos campaign. Mob attacks on monarchist newspapers in Rio in March, 1896, were only outward manifestations of the forces of nationalism at work in Brazil.[20] Euclides da Cunha calls the reaction of the masses to the defeats at Canudos "a common enough instance of collective psychology."[21]

Da Cunha's *Os Sertões* is much more than an excellent report on the military events of the Canudos War in 1896–1897. The author is portraying in miniature the vivid details of friction and violence occurring all along the northeastern frontier in the late nineteenth century—the confrontation between two widely differing Brazilian cultures, those of the coast and the interior. The poor *sertanejo* native had been abandoned and forgotten for centuries. Economically, socially, and politically he did not exist in any of the statistical reports on the state of the Republic emanating from the capital at Rio. And then suddenly, in 1896, a small group of these same *sertanejos* were galvanized into action by a prophet, Antônio Maciel, and appeared to threaten the very existence of the nation.[22] Antônio Maciel and his followers certainly represented an extreme manifestation of hatred toward the urban civilization of the coastal regions, but the same sort of distrust and resentment could be seen to a lesser degree over other areas of the *sertão*. The deeply religious and superstitious *sertanejos* could not comprehend the antireligious, positivist ideas that predominated in Rio, São Paulo, and other cities. The apocalyptic preachings of Antônio Maciel depicted the republican government as antichrist come to earth.[23] Nor could the men in Brazil's capital understand the reluctance of the *sertanejos* to leave their traditional way of life and accept all the "progress" that civilization had to offer them. Thus the impasse persisted.

The problem of conflicting cultures in Latin America was not original with Brazil in the 1890's. The schoolmaster president Domingo Sarmiento had written his own version of the struggle in his native Argentina in the first part of the nineteenth century. Sarmiento's *Civilización y Barbarie* reflected the same basic conflict between the new European-oriented elements of Argentina and the reticent gauchos, who clung to their barbaric ways.[24] To Sarmiento the gaucho was clearly the inferior element in the new Argentine society. Although he was physically superior, his stubborn reluctance to change was delaying Argentine progress. But his defeat was inevitable. When considering the ideal type of people upon which to build Argentine society, Sarmiento's contemporary Juan Alberdi chose not to educate the gaucho, but to eliminate him. Alberdi and Sarmiento both wanted European immigrants to come to people the land. They felt that these new groups would bring to Argentina agricultural skills and a tradition of self-sufficiency and national participation. In this way the outnumbered gauchos would be checked and pushed aside.[25]

Da Cunha, in Brazil, also viewed the outcome of the struggle as inevitable: "We are condemned to civilization. Either we shall progress or we shall perish, and our choice is clear."[26] But whereas Sarmiento looked upon the gaucho with contempt, da Cunha had discovered in the *sertão* a breed of men whom he admired. Physically strong, mentally alert, the *sertanejo* represented a group which had thrown off the veneer of European culture and had evolved its own rude native civilization. They desired only to be left alone. When the Republic exerted pressure upon them to conform to its norm, they reacted by striking out at the "foreigners" who threatened their traditional society. *Os Sertões* clearly accuses the civilized European portion of Brazilian society of being intruders and aggressors. Since the outcome of the conflict was inevitable, da Cunha believed that the only way for the Republic to justify its military aggressions was to bring the *sertanejo* into civilization, but learning from him instead of simply imparting its own culture upon him at bayonet point. Otherwise, force would be required in innumerable new Canudoses. And force had already failed as an effective means of controlling the situation; it had been necessary to eliminate the heroic *sertanejos* at Canudos to the last man.

Da Cunha did not doubt that the task of achieving national unity for Brazil would be long and arduous. Nor did the general public immediately accept the ideas of nationalism reflected in his work. Yet da Cunha did lay the groundwork for a modernist school of Brazilians who were to continue searching for new meanings and new beauty in their own native soil of Brazil. These included Heitor Villa-Lobos in the field of music,[27] Érico Veríssimo in the novel,[28] Cândido Portinari in painting,[29] Gilberto Freire in sociology,[30] and numerous others. They, like da Cunha, felt that if Brazilians could free themselves from slavish imitation of European doctrines and make Brazil, rather than France or England, their spiritual home, national unity would be possible. As for the value to be placed on the *sertanejo* in twentieth-century Brazilian society, da Cunha was certain that this group would be vitally important in Brazil's achieving a unity of race, sometime in the future. His own evaluation of the *sertanejo* follows:

> I did encounter in the backlands type [*sertanejo*] an ethnic subcategory already formed and one which, as a result of historical conditions, had been freed of the exigencies of a borrowed civilization such as would have hindered its definitive evolution. This is equivalent to saying that in that indefinable compound—the Brazilian—I came upon something that was stable, a point of resistance, . . . And it was natural enough that, once having admitted the bold and inspiring conjecture that we are destined to national unity, I should have seen in those sturdy *caboclos* the hardy nucleus of our future, the bedrock of our race.[31]

Notes

[1] Cf. A. Lalière, *Le café dans l'état de Saint Paul* (Paris, 1909), particularly the statistical appendices on coffee production and world prices broken down year by year from 1890 to 1909.

[2] Celso Furtado, *The Economic Growth of Brazil* (Berkeley, 1963), p. 143.

[3] Brazil's population had risen from an estimated 10,000,000 in the census of 1872, to over 17,318,000 by 1900. Cf. Herman G. James, *Brazil after a Century of Independence* (New York, 1925), pp. 255–290, especially p. 278.

[4] José Maria Bello, *A History of Modern Brazil, 1889–1964,* trans. by James L. Taylor (Stanford, 1966), pp. 172–207.

[5] James, *Brazil after a Century of Independence,* pp. 373–383.

[6] "General Cándido Mariano da Silva Rondón, a native of Mato Grosso, was a military engineer of great distinction. He guided Theodore Roosevelt on the famous trip in 1914 when the 'River of Doubt' (later named Rio Teodore Roosevelt) was discovered. . . . Rondón died in 1958 at the age of 92." See Maria Bello, *A History of Modern Brazil, 1889–1964,* p. 199.

[7] The Baron of Rio Branco, son of the Viscount of Rio Branco, became the Brazilian Minister of Foreign Affairs. He had already distinguished himself in the favorable settlement to Brazil of the Misiones territory, arbitrated by President Cleveland in 1895. He was likewise counsel in 1900 for Brazil in the boundary controversey with French Guiana, also settled favorably for Brazil, this time by the president of Switzerland. And in 1903, his negotiations with Bolivia led to the Treaty of Petrópolis, securing Brazil's position in the Acre territory of the Upper Amazon.

[8] João Lúcio de Azevedo, *A evolução do Sebastianismo* (Lisbon, 1947), pp. 119–120.

[9] Euclides da Cunha, *Rebellion in the Backlands (Os Sertões),* trans. by Samuel Putnam (Chicago, 1944), pp. 470–75.

[10] The first edition of *Os Sertões* was published in Rio de Janeiro in December, 1902.

[11] Braulio Sánchez-Saenz, "Euclides da Cunha: constructor de nacionalidad," *Agonía* (Buenos Aires, 1939), Vol. 4, pp. 52–56.

[12] Da Cunha, *Rebellion in the Backlands,* p. 153.

[13] The Brazilian historian José Maria Bello confirms da Cunha's observations: "The desire to efface the memory of the recent past naturally found expression in the classic manner of revolutionary demagoguery spellbound by its own words. Physical symbols of the past were obliterated; in official greetings, passé and poorly translated terms of the French Revolution like 'citizen' and 'health and fraternity' were adopted." Cf. Bello, *History of Modern Brazil, 1889–1964,* p. 66.

[14] Da Cunha, *Rebellion in the Backlands,* p. 161.

[15] Da Cunha, *Rebellion in the Backlands,* p. 278.

[16] Aira Kemiläinen, *Nationalism* (Jyvaskyla, 1964), p. 7.

[17] Kemiläinen, *Nationalism,* p. 9.

[18] These are 1) humanitarian nationalism; 2) Jacobin nationalism; 3) traditional nationalism; 4) liberal nationalism; 5) integral nationalism. Cf. Carlton J. H. Hayes, *The Historical Evolution of Modern Nationalism* (New York, 1931), pp. 5–223.

[19] Hayes, *The Historical Evolution of Modern Nationalism,* pp. 165–223.

[20] Da Cunha, *Rebellion in the Backlands,* pp. 278–279.

[21] Da Cunha, *Rebellion in the Backlands,* p. 227.

[22] Although dated, the only satisfactory biography of Antônio Maciel is R. B. Cunninghame-Graham's *Brazilian Mystic* (London, 1920). Mr. Cunninghame-Graham was a noted traveler of the early twentieth century who, unfortunately for this study, did not rely greatly on any original sources other than heavy borrowings from Euclides da Cunha's *Os Sertões.*

[23] Azevedo, *A evolução do Sebastianismo,* p. 119.

[24] Cf. Eugenio Villacana's foreword in Domingo F. Sarmiento, *Life in the*

Argentine Republic in the Days of the Tyrants, or Civilization and Barbarism (New York, 1961), pp. 5–6.

[25] Juan Bautista Alberdi, *Bases y puntos de partida para la organización política de la repúblic argentina* (Buenos Aires, 1943), pp. 75–76, 364.

[26] Da Cunha, *Rebellion in the Backlands*, p. 54.

[27] John Nist, *The Modernist Movement in Brazil* (Austin, 1967), pp. 69, 75, 88–89.

[28] Nist, *The Modernist Movement in Brazil*, p. 89; Nelson Werneck Sodré, *História da literatura brasileira* (Rio de Janeiro, 1940), p. 231.

[29] Nist, *Modernist Movement in Brazil*, pp. 60, 107.

[30] One of the best expressions of da Cunha's nativist ideas has come from the pen of another Brazilian sociologist, Gilberto Freyre. Freyre's *Casa grande e senzala*, first published in 1933, insisted that his country was not solely the product of Europe, but rather was shaped by a combination of European, African, and Amerindian cultures, which blended into a unique Brazilian civilization.

[31] Da Cunha, *Rebellion in the Backlands*, p. 481, NOTE V.

Richard A. Prêto-Rodas

The Development of Negritude in the Poetry
of the Portuguese Speaking World

In a colloquium devoted to Afro-French literature, which took place in Dakar in 1955, one of the speakers, Armand Guibert, began his lecture on negritude in French poetry with a reference to certain Brazilian writers of the nineteenth century.[1] According to the speaker, the Negro first became a subject of literary expression in the ringing verses of the young abolitionist Castro Alves, who evoked images of a sub-Sahara Africa of well-defined social units, whose members lived in close harmony with nature until they were abducted solely for reasons of color.

Although, as I intend to show, nineteenth-century Brazilian poets cannot be regarded as the pioneers of a fully developed negritude, it does seem somehow fitting that a modern Portuguese-language source should be recognized, since the first poetic expression of a black esthetic was made in the late Renaissance by Portugal's national poet, Luis de Camões. Flouting the prevailing Petrarchan canon of his time, which prescribed blond hair, blue or green eyes, and an alabaster neck for any proper poet's fancy, Camões sings the praises of his slave Bárbara, whose romantic slave he himself had become: ". . . black hair, black eyes . . . oh, blackness of love/an expression so sweet that the very snow would be happy to exchange its color for hers. . . ."[2] To be sure, such a candid avowal of the beauty of non-European women is exceptional

53

for the time and is not to be found again until its reappear-
ance in the last century in the poetry mentioned by Guibert.

   Nonetheless, the most committed abolition poetry of Brazil
saw in the Negro a victim of political injustice and tended to
idealize him in terms of European values rather than attempt
a specifically Afro-Brazilian point of view. Even more revealing is the fact that Negro and mulatto poets themselves, far
from writing as marginal members of a racially divided society, took great pains to conceal their background. Brazil's
major symbolist, João da Cruz e Sousa, himself the son of
African parents, indicates a longing for the white world in his
haunting evocations of ethereal, Nordic nights where Teu-
tonic women glide to the strains of violins. A study of his
poetry by Roger Bastide has revealed a deliberately aristocratic tone in which black imagery appears only to connote
feelings of terror, sinister forces, and melancholy.[3]

   A white esthetic is presumed even in a poem dedicated to
the Bahian *mulata* by Alexandre Melo Morais. When the poet
describes his subject, he somewhat apologetically says that
though her hair is as black as night her spirit is as white as
day.[4] At the same time, on the other shores of the Atlantic, the
black poet from São Tomé, Caetano de Costa Alegre, provides
an exotic image in his praise of an island beauty as a ". . .
walking sculpture carved from ebony glimpsed from afar."[5]

   Neither the idealized African of the abolitionist nor the
defensively described or exotic Negro of the nineteenth-
century poet writing for a white reader can have more than
a tenuous relation to the themes of modern negritude as I
shall outline them from contemporary Afro-Brazilian and
Afro-Portuguese writers. For their direct influences we must
look to three socio-literary movements of the twentieth century: Brazilian Modernism, Luso-Brazilian neo-Realism, and
the example of surrealist writers, principally the apostle of
French negritude, Aimé Césaire.[6]

With regard to Brazilian Modernism, the Semana de arte moderna in São Paulo in 1922 and its subsequent impact signaled a breaking away from a European literary context.[7] Such writers as Mário de Andrade and Jorge de Lima sought to underline cultural autonomy by emphasizing the non-European legacy towards the formation of a Brazilian character. For the past forty years there has been a growing reevaluation, especially of Africa's contribution to the country's cuisine, music, social customs, and language. With regard to language, one finds a common bond uniting contemporary poetry by Afro-Brazilians and Africans, in that both use a similar vocabulary liberally flavored with lexical items rarely found in traditional dictionaries.

Since 1922 and with the growth of Brazilian Modernism, the social novels of Brazilians and Lusitanian neo-Realism have further encouraged black writers to look to their immediate realities for literary material. For example, the Portuguese novelists, José Régio and Alves Redol have provided African readers with a technique for scrutinizing social ills which, for the Angolan and Mozambican writer, has become an examination of the relations between whites and blacks. Even more explicit has been the influence of Jorge Amado and José Lins do Rêgo. In Amado's novel *Jubiabá* many young Angolan and Cape Verdean writers have discovered a kindred world of *macumba*, struggle for social equality, and carefree disregard for bourgeois propriety, which provide alternatives to the decidedly European flavor of contemporary Portuguese writing.[8]

Of tremendous importance to all Negro writers both inside and outside the Portuguese-speaking world in their search for a nonconventional literary vehicle has been Surrealism and its subconscious realms, its audacious metaphors, and its general propensity for suggesting feelings and attitudes through nonlogical, strongly rhythmic expression. Thus, the first writer of negritude, Aimé Césaire, is for many critics primarily a craftsman of surrealistic technique and only incidently the major exponent of the black revolution in poetry.[9] Whichever emphasis one places on Césaire's poetry, a word regarding his *Cahier d'un retour au pays natal* is essential in any discussion of negritude.

Published in France in 1939, Césaire's lengthy exercise in Surrealism recreates his native Martinique as a living reminder of the oppressed state of the Antillean Negro. The poet tells how he himself, thanks to a superior education, had escaped this world until one day on a Paris streetcar he witnessed the taunts and gibes which several women directed to a tattered old Negro. For Césaire the moment took on the character of a religious conversion, for he became convinced that his own immunity from similar treatment would be possible only as long as he continued to blend into the dominant European background by acting like a white. From the experience he made a twofold resolve comprising a rejection and an affirmation, a resolve which has become the essence of modern negritude. Negatively, the poet would henceforth flaunt his identity as a nonwhite, repudiating the congeries of European values which he had assumed to counter his marginal significance as a black in a white society. Conversely, he would affirm his blackness, until now the badge of subjugation which had allowed his people to be conveniently cordoned off as an abject race.

For Césaire's colleague in letters, President Léopold Sédar Senghor of Senegal, the black must claim as his own the ideals of dignity and freedom, too long regarded as the domain of the European and his descendants: "We will choose the colonizer's own weapons [i.e., his language and his ideals] to assert our independence from him."[10] Both men avail themselves of Surrealism's daring innovations to reclassify all cultural values and argue for total ethnic relativism, thereby

dethroning occidental culture from its self-appointed supremacy as a measure and criterion for other peoples. Accordingly, Césaire cries out in his poem: "No race holds a
monopoly on beauty,"[11] a truism which, nevertheless, failed
to occur to the nineteenth-century Brazilians we have mentioned.

But to avoid absorption by the white value system, the
Negro poet, whatever his situation, must do more than simply
affirm his blackness: precisely *what* he hopes to affirm, however, is not clear. To be sure, as a literary point of departure
there is general agreement that negritude is definable in terms
of a highly emotional awareness of shared suffering and past
humiliation to be rectified by a strong assertion. But there is
little agreement concerning the content of such an assertion
other than the immediate fact of blackness.[12] Césaire's own
negritude is a mythical, literary construction combining the
idealized elements of a pre-European Africa where the black
lives in a state of nonrational, mystical union with rustling
forests and rushing waters.[13]

While such a semireligious negritude may be of some comfort to the Negro intellectual who lives in the insular society
of Martinique and Guadaloupe, it hardly serves the urban
writer who attempts to express himself as a black citizen of
cosmopolitan São Paulo or the boom towns of Angola and
Cabinda. We must remember, therefore, that negritude is a
theme susceptible of various interpretations, depending on
the poet's immediate situation.[14] Indeed, in a country with no
white power structure to rebel against, as in Ethiopia, there
cannot be a corresponding racial affirmation, and the theme
is nonexistent. Similarly, where cultural assimilation of African by European has never been a policy, such as in the
former English colonies, the movement is far weaker than in
French- and Portuguese-speaking areas where assimilation
has been or is presently being attempted.[15] The fluctuating

form which blackness takes both as a rejection of white, occidental values and as an assertion of negritude in Brazil, Cape Verde, and Portuguese Africa should therefore be construed as variations on a very elusive theme.[16]

In Brazilian negritude one finds little mention of the "Mother Africa" mystique of Aimé Césaire. Careful distinction should be made between blackness and what the French anthropologist Roger Bastide has called "literary Africanitude."[17] The absence of legal barriers regulating racial contacts and the *mestiço* ancestry of many Brazilians simply render impossible any movement such as Africanitude with its implications of antagonistic, cultural polarities. However, tolerance regarding racial origins in Brazil is not always matched by a corresponding tolerance in reference to racial appearance. The last forty years have seen a growing protest on the part of black Brazilians, who refuse to accept a veiled official policy that would consign them to a subaltern role while a long historical process leads to the day when their descendants, properly "bleached out," may aspire to full social equality. Negritude in modern Brazilian poetry is, therefore, an aspect of a general socio-political movement, which has given rise to such organizations as the União Negra Brasileira, O Movimento Brasileiro contra o Preconceito da Côr, and A União dos Homens de Côr. These and similar bodies sponsor newspapers, art shows, and even beauty contests to alter the popular view of the docile black who was yesterday's slave, is today's servant, and eventually will become tomorrow's rarely acknowledged ancestor.[18]

The Afro-Brazilian writer Guerreiro Ramos argues against the tacit opinion that white is better than black on patriotic grounds. Those who welcome the bleaching out of the African component are, he claims, guilty of a supine, colonial mentality, for they passively allow a European model to serve as a national image.[19] Similarly, the founder of the Teatro Experimental do Negro, Abdias do Nascimento, describes his work as an effort to "... give value to and exalt the contribution of the African to the growth of Brazil ... while exposing the fraud of Brazilian whiteness: a people of colored origin who officially pretend to be white."[20] Their position is that racial assimilation is mulattoization rather than progressive Aryanization. Whatever the term, there is clearly involved a denial of an exclusively European past and a concomitant affirmation of African origins. Their purpose, however, is not to polarize the races but simply to vindicate the common dignity of all races in a *mestiço* society.

In the works of two prominent Afro-Brazilian poets, Carlos de Assunção and Oswaldo do Camargo, the reader immediately notes that the past weighs heavily on the black poet in Brazil. In his long poem "Protesto," de Assunção evokes the shades of his slave forebears for a discussion on "... bitter topics/like chains and bonds/ ... /which today are invisible/though they exist/binding the arms, the thoughts/the feet/the dreams/of each man who lives/like myself as a stepchild of our country."[21] Reinforcing the notion of a frustrated membership in a national community, he proceeds to address his fellow, nonblack citizen: "Pity does not interest me, brother./I want something better./I want simply to live somewhere else/besides in the cellar of our society."[22] The same preoccupation with past wrongs and present inequality permeates Oswaldo do Camargo's poetry, though his tone is far more bellicose, as we can see in his exhortation to the black reader that comprises the poem "Atitude": "... cast aside your tame glances, your timidity, and your eternally happy smile .../be hard, black man/hard/like the post on which they lashed you a thousand times./Be black, black, black,/ marvelously black."[23]

The growing appeal which an African ancestry has for a mixed society is dramatically evident in recent writings from

Cape Verde. This archipelago, situated in the south Atlantic midway between Portugal and Brazil, has long boasted a surprisingly large number of writers, some white, others black, but mostly *mestiço*, as is the case with the vast majority of the islands' more than 150,000 inhabitants. Until recent years, though, most writers ignored their racial ancestry and devoted their talents to academic topics and an occasional lament prompted by the harsh social and economic conditions which afflict Cape Verde. To be sure, the *Almanac Luso-Africano*, the first journal edited in the port city of São Vicente in 1894, referred to the vestigial Africanisms in the popular dialect and in certain customs; but the general tendency was to emphasize the European substratum of a Creole culture.[24]

With the advent of Brazilian Modernism and Portuguese neo-Realism, more and more Cape Verde writers are referring to the African character of their people, if only in terms of those socio-economic realities that recall the slave society of the past. For example, in 1932 the poet Pedro Monteiro Cardoso directed a poem in dialect to the white minority in which he says: "You are rich and I am poor./You are white and I am black./Neither color represents a virtue, neither a defect."[25] Recent poets have more strongly aligned themselves with Brazilian negritude. In 1953 Jorge Barbosa related his tiny islands to their giant brother across the sea in a long eulogy, "Você, Brasil," where he muses: "Both our souls still feel the poignant memories/of the savannas of Africa."[26] Nonetheless, as late as 1953, the Angolan nationalist Mário de Andrade excluded the Cape Verdeans from his anthology of Negro poetry in Portuguese. Five years later, however, he did include Cape Verdeans in a second edition, in recognition of the increasing identity, which many of the younger poets are voicing, with the emerging nations of Africa.[27]

Whether negritude in Cape Verdean poetry will transcend its present concentration on anguished memories and present

humiliations is doubtful. The islands' severely limited resources seem to preclude any major social improvement. Perhaps for this reason, young intellectuals in growing numbers
are joining their future to the independence movement of
nearby Guinea on the African mainland. Even so, the over-
whelmingly Creole character of the populace with its un-
mistakably Portuguese subculture would seem to warrant
the distinction—which we have already made in the case of
Brazilian blacks—between a simple assertion of negritude
and the more elaborate construct that is Africanitude.

No such distinction is necessary as we examine the form
which negritude is taking in the rapidly growing number of
writers from São Tomé, Guinea, and, especially, Angola and
Mozambique. What the black man rejects and what he hopes
to affirm are both clearly defined in these areas, where a social
system for African masses is imposed by a European minority.
Not content with evoking bitter recollections of past and present subjugation, most Afro-Portuguese poets are committed
to political separation.[28] It is not by accident that fifteen out
of eighteen poets included in a recent anthology are presently
in prison or in exile.[29]

The dean of Luso-African negritude was a mulatto intellectual from the island of São Tomé, Dr. José Francisco Tenreiro. The social abyss which, despite the absence of official
legislation, prevents the non-white from gaining full accep-
tance in Portuguese Africa represented for the mulatto Tenreiro a personal cleavage as well. His dedicatory verses to his
first book, *Ilha de Nome Santo*, written in Lisbon in 1942, are
revealing: "To my mother: Between us there are thousands of
miles; between us there is a race."[30] In a poem dedicated to
his black mother, the writer decries a world where she can
see her descendants prosper only by losing their racial identity
with her: "Oh mother of blacks and *mestiços* and grand-
mother of whites."[31]

Even the totally Europeanized African must admit that his is a fanciful world. In the poem "Canção de um negro com alma de branco" by the popular Angolan lawyer-poet Gerardo Bessa Victor, we read of a young African who is rudely jolted after years of city life with Europeans when he tenderly expresses love for the daughter of his white godmother. When she repels him with "You silly black," he has no defense but to repeat in hurt confusion: "But I have a white soul."[32] In Bessa Victor's best known poem, "O Menino negro não entrou na roda," it is implied that racial division is in itself artificially induced. Thus, when a white mother scolds her children for inviting an African child to join in their games, there is born that notion of "otherness" which becomes prejudice for the white and alienation for the black.[33]

As a reaction to an imposed European standard for social acceptability we may cite the Whitmanesque odes of José Craveirinha, a journalist from Mozambique. In a proud "song-to-myself" entitled "Manifesto," he glories in his black, kinky hair, his full lips, and the smooth ebony color of his lithe body.[34] In another ode, dedicated to Africa, he points out the defects of the West and suggests that Africa, perhaps, has something to offer. Thus, he repudiates the paternalism of those who, he says, love the African with the ". . . intolerant love of their Gospels,/the mystique of glass beads and gunpowder,/the logic of machine gun chatter,/and songs from lands we do not know."[35] For Craveirinha the European's superior technology is a Frankenstein's monster, which indeed permits him to master nature but only at the cost of dehumanizing himself. The poet's indictment of the West is a sweeping one as he describes a culture whose great thinkers and scientists are counterbalanced by such doubtful contributions to the world as the electric chair, the efficiency of Buchenwald, the Inquisition, and " . . . a bird heavy with the egg which it later hatched on the warm nest of Hiroshima."[36]

Along with many of his African colleagues, the poet offers to temper the white man's abuse of nature and, indirectly, of himself, with a generous dose of the African's animistic oneness with his surroundings. In a similar vein his fellow Mozambican, Virgílio de Lemos, offers to cure a Europe, sick ". . . with its senile sarcasm, toothless dialectics, and aborted super-existencialism [sic] . . . ," by prescribing some of the African's frank sensuality and the " . . . drumbeats of my euforia [sic] . . . ."[37] Almost thirty years ago Tenreiro sounded a similar note in his poem "Mãos" when he wrote: "Wise black hands/ that invented neither writing nor the compass . . . but from the earth, from each tree, from the water and the tom-tom beat of the heart/created religion and art, religion and love."[38]

But a cultural partnership between European and African is impossible as long as the black remains little more than a source of cheap labor for a colonial economy. It follows that a central theme in Afro-Portuguese negritude is one of revolt and indignation, as we can infer from the series of jabbing verse questions comprising most of a poem by the Angolan Antônio Jacinto: "Who weeds and gets paid in disdain/ spoiled flour, spoiled fish/shoddy cloth, fifty brass coins/'A beating if you answer back'/Who?—Who makes the corn grow/the orange trees blossom/Who?—Who provides the cash for bossman to buy/machines, women, cars/and bronze Negro heads to adorn the hoods/Who allows the white to prosper/have a big belly—have money?—Who? . . ." And he affirms his telluric unity with his land as all of nature responds: "You, monangamba! [contract laborer]."[39]

From outrage to rebellion is a small step, and there is no dearth of revolutionary poetry against "them": "Oh, THEY will change, but only/when fear overcomes THEM . . ." cries Virgílio de Lemos.[40] Equally noteworthy, though, is the absence of hatred for the individual Portuguese soldier. Rui Nogar movingly describes the heroism born of hysteria of the poor European villager sent to fight other villagers for reasons of ". . . a hatred not his own . . ." until he too is killed.[41] Indeed, there are many poems containing a wealth of metaphors that connote a day of childlike unconcern for race and social standing when harmony will reign: "Children will be children/black, golden, and white/like the varied petals of a single flower" says the exiled Cape Verdean Onésimo da Silveira.[42] And Mozambique's foremost woman poet Noêmia de Sousa, alternates the militant ring of her revolutionary verses with reminiscences of a childhood in a poor neighborhood where the children of immigrant whites, blacks, mulattoes, and East Indians all played in carefree camaraderie.

I should like to close by reading in the original a short poem by José Craveirinha, "Grito Negro,"[43] which may serve as a synthesis of Afro-Portuguese negritude. The poet, incidentally, is a master in creating the verbal magic that some Africanists claim is a distinguishing characteristic of Africans writing in western tongues.[44] By employing the suggestive power of a metaphor identifying himself with coal, the poet shouts his color, his unity with his native land, his exploited existence at the hand of the white, and his determination to direct his strength toward liberating himself, his land, and, ironically, his white overseer, whom he calls "brother." In all but two verses Craveirinha achieves the percussive background of the throbbing *batuque* through repetition of the nasal termination "-ão."

> Eu sou carvão!
> E tu arrancas-me brutalmente do chão
> e fazes-me tua mina, patrão.
> Eu sou carvão!
> E tu acendes-me, patrão,
> para te servir eternamente como fôrça motriz
> mas eternamente não, patrão.
> Eu sou carvão

e tenho que arder sim;
queimar tudo com a fôrça da minha combustão.
Eu sou carvão;
tenho que arder na exploração
arder até as cinzas da maldição
arder vivo como alcatrão, meu irmão,
até não ser mais a tua mina, patrão.
Eu sou carvão.
Tenho que arder
Queimar tudo com o fogo da minha combustão.
Sim!
Eu sou o teu carvão, patrão.[43]

Notes

[1] Armand Guibert, "Les poètes de la Négritude: Thèmes et Techniques," *Actes du Colloque sur la littérature africaine d'expression française* (Dakar, 1965), pp. 219–227.

[2] "Olhos . . . / prêtos e cansados . . . / Pretidão de amor / . . . Prêtos os cabelos . . . / Tão doce a figura, / que a neve lhe jura / Que trocara a côr. . . ."—Luis de Camões, *Obras completas*, Vol. 1 (Lisbon, 1962), p. 93. [All translations are the author's.]

[3] Roger Bastide, *A poesia afro-brasileira* (São Paulo, 1943), pp. 88–99.

[4] "Se a noite são meus cabelos / O dia é meu coração."—Alexandre Melo Morais, "A mulata," in *Antologia da canção brasileira* (São Paulo, 1963), pp. 176–179.

[5] Caetano de Costa Alegre, "Visão" in *Poetas e contistas africanos*, ed. João Alves das Neves (São Paulo, 1963), p. 29.

[6] Gerald M. Moser, "African Literature in the Portuguese Language," *The Journal of General Education*, Vol. 12 (1962), pp. 270–304; Norman Araújo, *A Study of Cape Verdean Literature* (Boston, 1966), p. 83.

[7] For a good study of the "Semana da arte moderna" and its consequences, see Wilson Martins, *A literatura brasileira, O Modernismo* (1916–1945), Vol. 6 (São Paulo, 1965).

[8] For an example, see Mário Antônio's "Canto de farra": "Quando li Jubiabá/me cri Antônio Balduino . . ." in *100 Poemas* (Luanda, 1963), p. 46.

[9] See the introduction by André Breton to the bilingual edition of Aimé Césaire's *Cahier d'un retour au pays natal*, trans. Lionel Abel and Ivan Goll (New York, 1947).

[10] Léopold Sédar Senghor, "Négritude et civilization de l'universel," *Présence Africaine*, Vols. 45–48 (1963), pp. 8–13. Future references to *Présence Africaine* are abbreviated: PA.

[11] Aimé Césaire, *Cahier d'un retour au pays natal* (Paris, 1956), p. 83.

For negritude as a part of the modern reclassification of all values, see Thomas Melone, *De la Négritude dans la littérature négro-africaine* (Paris, 1962), pp. 38–39.

[12] See L-V Thomas, "Panorame de la Négritude," *Actes du Colloque sur la littérature africaine d'expression française* (Dakar, 1965), pp. 72–97.

[13] Césaire, *Cahier d'un retour au pays natal*, p. 49: "A force de penser au Congo/je suis devenu un Congo bruissant de forêts et de fleuves. . . ."

[14] Thomas, in "Panorame de la Négritude," p. 46, insists that the character of literary negritude is essentially situational.

[15] See the introduction to the Penguin Books edition of *Modern Poetry from Africa* (Baltimore, 1963), pp. 18–19.

[16] See Roger Bastide, "Variations sur la Négritude," *PA*, Vol. 36 (1961), pp. 7–17.

[17] Bastide, "Variations sur la Négritude," p. 8.

[18] For a survey of the Afro-Brazilian socio-political movement, see Bastide, "Variations sur la Négritude"; Thomas Blair, "Mouvements afro-brésiliens de libération de la période esclavagiste à nos jours," *PA*, Vol. 53 (1965), pp. 96–101; and, in the same volume, Octavio Iânni, "Race et classe au Brésil," pp. 182–199; Fernando Henrique Cardoso, "Le préjugé de couleur au Brésil," pp. 120–129.

[19] Roger Bastide, "Variations sur la Négritude," p. 10.

[20] Abdias do Nascimento, *Dramas para negros, prólogo para brancos* (Rio de Janeiro, 1961), p. 21.

[21] ". . . sôbre coisas amargas: sobre grilhões e correntes/que no passado eram visíveis/ que no presente são invisíveis;/invisíveis mas existentes,/ nos braços, no pensamento,/nos passos/nos passos, nos sonhos/ na vida/ de cada um dos que vivem/juntos comigo enjeitados da Pátria."—Carlos de Assunção in *nouvelle somme de poésie du monde noir*, Vol. 57 of *PA*, separata series [n.d.]. The title is also given in English, Spanish, and Portuguese.

[22] "Piedade não me interessa . . ./Eu quero coisa melhor/Eu não quero mais viver/no porão da sociedade—Assunção, *nouvelle somme de poésie du monde noir*, p. 510.

[23] "Deixa essa mansidão nos olhos, essa delicadeza/e esse eterno riso jovial . . ./Sê duro, ó negro, duro,/como o poste em que mil vezes te chicotearam! /Sê negro, negro, negro,/Maravilhosamente negro."—Oswaldo do Camargo, "Atitude," in *Convite à Negritude* (São Paulo, 1965), p. 44.

[24] See Norman Araújo, *A Study of Cape Verdean Literature* (Boston, 1966), p. 92.

[25] "Nhô ê rico mi ê prôbre./Nhô ê branco mi ê prêto,/Calquer dés ê ca grandeza,/Calquer dés ê ca defêto"—Araújo, *A Study of Cape Verdean Literature*, p. 58.

[26] "Ambas . . . /sentindo ainda saudades antigas/dos sertões africanos." Jorge Barbosa, "Você, Brazil"—*Caderno de um ilhéu: Poemas* (Lisbon, 1956), p. 58.

[27] *Caderno da poesia negra de expressão portuguêsa*, ed. Mário de Andrade (Lisbon, 1953); *Antologia da poesia negra de expressão portuguêsa*, ed. Mário de Andrade (Paris, 1958).

[28] Mário de Andrade, "Littérature et nationalisme en Angola," *PA*, Vol. 41 (1962), p. 95.

[29] See *nouvelle somme de poésie du monde noir*, pp. 437–500.

[30] "Mãe: entre nós: milhas!/Entre nós: uma raça!/Contudo/este livro é para ti . . ."—José Francisco Tenreiro, *Obra poética* (Lisbon, 1967), p. 37.

[31] See "Nós, Mae" in Tenreiro, *Obra poética*, pp. 98–101.

[32] Geraldo Bessa Victor, *Cubata abandonada* (Braga, 1966), pp. 27–30.

[33] Geraldo Bessa Victor, *Mucanda* (Braga, 1965), pp. 13–14.

[34] José Craveirinha, "Manifesto" in *nouvelle somme de poésie du monde noir*, Vol. 57 of *PA*, separata series [n.d.], pp. 474–475.

[35] "A única verdade dos seus evangelhos/A mística das suas missangas e da sua pólvora/a lógica das suas rajadas de metralhadora/ . . . e as canções das terras que eu não conheço."—Craveirinha in *nouvelle somme de poésie du monde noir*, pp. 470–71.

[36] ". . . e emprenharam o pássaro que fez o chôco/sobre o ninho morno de Hiroxima." Craveirinha in *nouvelle somme de poésie du monde noir*, p. 488.

[37] "Teu sarcasmo senil/tua lógica desdentada . . ./teu abortado super-existencialismo" as opposed to " . . . os tans-tans da minha euforia. . . ."—Virgílio de Lemos, "Teus blocos de gêlo, Europa!" *nouvelle somme de poésie du monde noir*, Vol. 57 of *PA*, separata series [n.d.], pp. 486–88.

[38] "Mãos pretas e sábias que nem inventaram a escrita nem a rosa-dos-ventos/mas que da terra, da árvore, da água, e do coração tan-tan/criasteis religião e arte, religião e amor."—Tenreiro, *Obra poética*, pp. 89–90 cf. Césaire's countering the white's *raison* with the black's *folie* in Aimé Césaire, *Cahier d'un retour au pays natal*, pp. 42–43. For an analysis of the pathos and sympathy of negritude as virtues countering the Occident's stress on efficiency and technological expertise, see Melone, *De la Négritude dans la littérature négro-africaine*, pp. 70–88; Guibert, "Les Poètes de la Négritude: Thèmes et Techniques," p. 220; W. A. Jeanpierre, "La Négritude vue par un afro-américain," *PA*, Vol. 30 (1959), pp. 101–117.

[39] "Quem capina e em paga recebe desdém/fubá pôdre, peixe pôdre,/ panos ruins, cinquenta angolare/*porrada se refilares?*/ Quem?/ Quem faz o milho crescer/e os laranjais florescer/-Quem? Quem dá dinheiro para o patrão comprar/máquinas, carros, senhoras/ e cabeças de prêtos para os motores? Quem faz o branco prosperar,/ter a barriga grande—ter dinheiro?/-Quem?/ . . . "Monangambeeee! . . ."—Costa Alegre, *Poetas e contistas africanos*, pp. 42–43.

[40] "Oh, ÊLES hão-de mudar, mas sòmente/quando o medo se apoderar DÊLES. . . ."—De Lemos, "Terceiro Poema do guerreiro Xangam que há em mim," *nouvelle somme de poésie du monde noir*, Vol. 57 of *PA*, separata series [n.d.], p. 488.

[41] Rui Nogar, "Poesia do guerreiro involuntário," *nouvelle somme de poésie du monde noir*, p. 482.

[42] "As crianças serão crianças! /Negras, louras, e brancas/Serão pétalas da mesma flor . . ."—Onésimo da Silveira, in "Hora grande," *nouvelle somme de poésie du monde noir*, p. 456. The poet, who lives in mainland China here

expresses the orthodox Marxist view of negritude as an expression of technical backwardness and divisive with regard to a more universal form of human solidarity. See Thomas, "Panorame de la Négritude," p. 81.

[43] José Craveirinha, "Grito Negro," *Poetas e contistas africanos,* ed. by João Alves das Neves (São Paulo, 1963), p. 60.

[44] See Janheinz Jahn, "Sur la littérature africaine," *PA,* Vols. 45–48 (1963), pp. 151–162.

Comments BY FLORENE J. DUNSTAN

Dr. Prêto-Rodas reveals the search of the Portuguese-speaking Negro to find his own identity, to express himself, and to develop his own esthetic. I read the paper with great interest and, of course, thought of parallels in Spanish American poetry. In a collection of poems entitled, *Poesía Afrocubana,*[1] Ramón Guirao includes thirteen poets. In his introduction he states that the poetry *de tema negro* is the most genuine manifestation of Cuba's artistic sensitiveness, and cites Guillermo Díaz Plaja: "Afro-Cuban poetry elevates an entire continent."[2] The anthology edited by H. R. Hayes, *Twelve Spanish American Poets,* includes Nicolás Guillén,[3] a mulatto, the leader and most important poet of the Afro-Cuban school. Throughout his poems, there is a bitter strain of social protest and social satire. Steeped in Negro folklore and in contemporary dance rhythms of Cuba, he has turned popular ballads and *sones* into poetry, at once simple and serious in intention.

Guillén's work is considered to have significance in giving artistic form to the contribution of the Negroes and mulattoes to the culture of Latin America. It has also acted as a stimulus to members of the Negro race throughout the Caribbean area. Some of his best known poems, set to music, bear a close relation to the American blues. One of these, "Sensemayá," is an adaptation of a traditional magical incantation to protect a man who is killing a snake. The African words of the refrain are used for their sound value—a typical device of Cuban poets. Most of these words have already lost their meaning for the modern Cuban, but they live on in popular tradition as the nonsense refrains of some game songs do in English.

The majority of poems with a black esthetic are from Cuba, although some have been written in other countries where there are many Negro inhabitants, such as Panama and Ecuador.

The word "negritude" does not appear in the standard dictionaries; nor could I find its equivalent, *negrismo*, in any Spanish dictionary. I thought I knew what it meant, so that I was greatly interested in the assertion by Dr. Prêto-Rodas that its meaning was changing and elusive. I called Mrs. Grace Perry, registrar at Spelman College and a close personal friend of mine, and told her that I was to discuss a paper on "negritude" in the poetry of the Portuguese-speaking world and that I was interested in knowing whether it is an active word in the present-day student's vocabulary. "Oh, yes indeed, I've heard the word used many times recently, but I don't think you will find it in any dictionary. It is a basic word in the Black Power movement." Worried as I was by my lack of information and intrigued by the many variations of the word, I then went to the Trevor Arnett Library at Atlanta University Center, which is composed of five outstanding Negro colleges.[4]

One of the librarians, a young woman named Miss Lillian Miles, directed me to materials and discussed with me the ideas of negritude that exist among young Negroes today. She said that with all of them the basic note was the assertion of blackness and the necessity for pride in it. Some of the young generation wish to stress blackness and cut all ties with white people. She said that she had first heard the word "negritude" in 1960 in connection with Césaire and Senghor. When I questioned her about negritude in America today, Miss Miles said, "We use the word often, but not exactly as Césaire did, and even among Negroes there is a difference of opinion as to its meaning." She stated that all agree that the Negro must take pride in his origins, that he must feel a sense of strength and beauty in his blackness; but some advocate separation entirely from the white race, and some go so far as to advocate violence to establish the superiority of blackness.

Even among writers a wide range of opinion exists. The very illuminating *Negro Digest*, in the January, 1968, issue reports a survey made recently by that magazine. In the introduction the editors stated that, since there is such a wide divergence of ideas among black writers as to their role in society, in the Black Revolution, and as artists, the *Negro Digest* had decided to poll thirty-eight black writers, some famous and some unknown, as to influences in their lives, particularly literary influences. They were also asked what they thought of the future of the literary school which holds that there must be a black esthetic if a black writer is to achieve anything. Gwendolyn Brooks, the only black poet to be honored with a Pulitzer prize, when asked her idea about that school of writers wanting to establish a "black esthetic," replied, "Certainly, there is a future. It is a most exciting concept."[5] Another writer, Addison Gayle, Jr., does not see any future for such writers. He said, "The black esthetic has always been a part of the lives of black people."[6] Another, Cyrus Colter, said, "Yes—and I like the way the question is put. Its implication is not a foreclosure of choice on the part of the black writer, for I don't think he should be persuaded at all costs that he must write only about and for Negroes."[7] The opinion of the writers seemed to be about evenly divided, with the more mature writers insisting that a black esthetic is not the goal for which they should strive, and the younger ones feeling that "it is the wave of the future."

Dr. Prêto-Rodas evidently had access to many unusual sources, and his presentation to us of this material opens up a phase of cultural relations which will be a rewarding study to anyone who wishes to pursue it.

Notes

[1] Ramón Guirao, *Orbita de la poesía afrocubana* (Havana, 1938).

[2] Guirao, Introduction to *Orbita de la poesía afrocubana*, p. xii.

[3] H. R. Hayes, *Twelve Spanish American Poets* (New Haven, 1943), pp. 218–237.

[4] Dr. Hugh Gloster, President of Morehouse College, one of those in the Atlanta University Center, has been particularly interested in the Negro in literature, especially in North America, and has written extensively on the

theme of the Negro as a writer and as the theme of literature. Atlanta University has a large special collection of books and manuscripts on all phases of Negro life. Preliminary planning has already been made to establish a program at the Center which will lead first to a minor and then to a major in Afro-American studies, and I was told that this means all of the Americas, not merely North America.

[5] Gwendolyn Brooks in "A Survey," *Negro Digest* (January, 1968), p. 29.
[6] Addison Gayle, Jr., "A Survey," p. 32.
[7] Cyrus Colter, "A Survey," p. 34.

Roberto Esquenazi-Mayo

Social Aspects of the Contemporary Spanish American Novel

ALFONSO REYES once wrote that Spanish American literature is the reflection of the social life of an entire region. The
outstanding Venezuelan critic, novelist, and statesman Arturo
Uslar Pietri pointed out in his prologue to *Prize Stories from
Latin America* that the social psychologist could find a source
of data of incalculable value in the selections included in this
book. It has been said, at times with deliberate persistence,
that all literary works reflect social conditions. There are
writers who undertake their work with that purpose in mind.
Balzac longed to reflect an entire period of French history.
And I do not believe that only realists and naturalists should
be included in this category. Many writers, including Galdós,
Unamuno, Germán Arciniegas, Alfonso Reyes, Eduardo Ba-
rrios, Jorge Luis Borges, Eduardo Mallea, and Juan Rulfo,
have made, in their own manner, contributions that help us
interpret the social and cultural state of Spanish America.
Even poets like Nicolás Guillén and Pablo Neruda have pub-
licly declared their "social function." Albert Camus insisted
that all responsible writers should adopt a stand on the social
problems of their time. Nor did William Faulkner evade that
intimate and mysterious integration that consists of the interpretation of what is clearly social by aesthetic means. Jorge
Mañach revealed his sense of social responsibility when he
wrote about Gabriela Mistral: "And it would be fitting to

73

point out this interpenetration of the spiritual and terrestrial in her poetry about nature, which includes not only the verses that interpret the landscape, but also the scattered prose in which Gabriela has eulogized *humble things and occupations*."[1]

A number of studies on European literatures exist in which emphasis is placed on the relationship between the social and purely artistic without the former excluding the latter, or vice versa. In Spanish American literature it is difficult at times to classify an author. Do all critics agree on what Sarmiento's *Facundo* really is? And what about Montalvo or Martí? About González Prada and Rodó? However, it does not seem to me necessary to sacrifice esthetic sensitivity in order to emphasize moral or political concerns, as these men have done. The austerity of the artist may give rise to concern about, and criticism of, national life, which, in my judgement, is what literary works have been mistakenly emphasizing in order to complement statistics and technical reports. Perhaps there has been more insistence on the apparent and obvious in the novel than on the substance and technique.

But it so happens that, in spite of the will of the scholar, there are events that are intimately linked. Is it possible to understand the novel of the Mexican Revolution, even attempt a classification of it, without first evaluating the objectives of the Revolution and its development, victories, and failures? Can one understand Martín Luis Guzmán without reading *La querella de México*? A literary work is not a statistical study, nor is it useful for the statistics of economists and sociologists, but it does not alarm me that from its study—without excluding the essentially esthetic—some sound conclusions are derived that enhance our knowledge of a historical period. "El matadero," by Echeverría, is one of the many examples that could be cited. One does not know whether to admire the descriptive ability of the author or to react violently against the bloody regime of Rosas. In the United States the young critics have been able to point out both the esthetic and the social values in Spanish American literature. The new crop of United States critics show not only interest but also thought and discernment in their evaluation of the purely esthetic and the fundamentally socioeconomic. In a way John Oliver Killens, one of the most outstanding United States novelists and dramatists of the Negro race, summarizes better than anyone this balanced approach when he states that a Negro artist, if he wishes to remain an artist, must reflect the feelings of his people.[2]

About the first forty years of the twentieth century indicate a very special characteristic of the Spanish American novel: "Nature" seems to be the protagonist. The jungle, the Andes, the highland plains, and the desert capture the imagination of the author. Nevertheless, although nature predominates in the style of *La Vorágine* of the Colombian José Eustasio Rivera (1888–1928) or in *Doña Bárbara* of the Venezuelan Rómulo Gallegos (born 1884), one notes, feels, and almost senses the preoccupation that they have for social themes. Although both describe the landscape brilliantly, they nevertheless seek a definition of *lo nacional.*

In Spanish America there has been a constant search for a definition of a "national identity," or a "national conscience." It is easy to see this search not only in the novel but especially in the essay. Writers such as José Enrique Rodó of Uruguay or Octavio Paz of Mexico ask themselves identical questions, although they do not arrive at the same conclusions. The Ecuadorian Jorge Icaza in his novel *Huasipungo* also undertakes a search for a national identity, but he does it undoubtedly with a totally different technique from that of Rodó and Paz, and he does it in the novel instead of in the essay and in poetry.

The exploited Indian, the Negro, and the *cholo*, appear as

important elements in the literature of Spanish America, from *Raza de bronce* by the Bolivian Alcides Arguedas to the most recent novels of the Mexicans Sainz, Prado, and Fuentes.

Spanish America has not been wanting in the production of novels of the subconscious, especially during the last fifteen years. Nor has it been remiss in experimentation. *Cambio de piel* by Carlos Fuentes, *Rayuela* by Julio Cortázar, *La ciudad y los perros* by Mario Vargas Llosa, and *Cien años de soledad* by Gabriel García Márquez are good examples of experiments already acclaimed by international critics. Cortázar, for example, has succeeded in assimilating Joyce, Kafka, and Faulkner, and has created something uncommon in the literature of the Spanish language. Not only has he attempted to investigate *lo nacional*, but he has also opened new avenues in style with his daring and refined prose, with his *jitanjáforas*, which in a way remind us of what Lewis Carroll wrote in English in his *Jabberwocky*. In a similar manner, Juan Rulfo in *Pedro Páramo* tries to free himself from the shackles of words in order to seek the supernatural and the infinite. Mario Benedetti in *La tregua* conceives characters inevitably Uruguayan, but also universal in that they represent the frustrations of man in a society paralyzed by bureaucracy. Although Jorge Luis Borges, a candidate for the Nobel Prize for Literature, is not a novelist in the strictest sense of the word, he has, without doubt, left an indelible mark on prose and on world literature. The French critic Roger Caillois wrote about Borges that "the importance and the originality of Jorge Luis Borges in contemporary literature are very well recognized at this time."[3] Characteristics that have elevated him to a very special place among the writers of the Spanish language are his precise use of the language, his erudition that is manifest even in poetry, his cosmic concept of time, his concept of the universe as if it were a gigantic labyrinth, and his conviction that time is nothing but a dream and that he himself and his work are part of an insatiable world ("Más allá de este afán y de este verso/Me aguarda inagotable el Universo").[4]

Nevertheless, even with all his experiments, his incursions in styles, themes, and genres, the social element—the search for an explanation and a solution to exploitation, violence, and instability—predominates.

Perhaps no one has cultivated "the novel of violence," which is essentially political, social, and moral as well as the Colombian Eduardo Caballero Calderón (born 1910). He has distinguished himself as one of the most notable prose stylists of the twentieth century. His complete works have been published in three volumes by Editorial Bedout of Medellín, Colombia. Each volume has some six hundred pages. The most extraordinary characteristic of this edition is the variety of themes and literary genres that Caballero Calderón has cultivated. He has written about the destiny of man in the New World; he has described Castile and has commented on the history of his country. In more than twenty-five years of literary activity, he has not relaxed his stylistic impetus. He established himself firmly as a novelist in 1940 when he published *Tipacoque*. In this work, at times with the simplicity of Azorín and sometimes with the flowing eloquence of Ortega y Gasset, Caballero Calderón summarizes his childhood experiences in the fertile lands of the interior. His novel *El buen salvaje*, which won the Nadal Prize for 1966, is an excellent example of his prismatic production, for he deviates from what he had published until then to make a notable entry into the field of the psychological novel. But *Manuel Pacho* and *El Cristo de espaldas* are the novels that place him among the most important novelists in Spanish America.

In a country where good writers are a national trait, statesmen like Alberto Lleras Camargo and Eduardo Santos, diplomats and scholars like Germán Arciniegas, short-story writers like Hernando Téllez and Próspero Morales Pradilla, and

novelists like García Márquez have all gone beyond their
national frontiers and have become universal writers. Among
them Caballero Calderón is outstanding. The Colombian
critic Juan Lozano y Lozano has said that in the works of
Caballero Calderón "the unity and strength of a spirit come
together. . . the presentation and evaluation of the problems
of man and contemporary society."[5] One of the great preoccu-
pations of Caballero Calderón is the man in the New World
vis à vis the European. What is Latin America and where is
she going? Is it possible that she will develop her own character and at the same time retain the best of the Spanish cultural traditions? Is it the destiny of Colombia to live under
the constant threat of violent politics? These are some of the
questions that Caballero Calderón tries to answer in his novels
and essays. When in *Suramérica, tierra del hombre* he asks
himself: "Does the South American exist?," he answers cate-
gorically: "One must not lose sight of the fact that the spirit
of the liberators was South American before it was Argentine,
Chilean, Colombian, or Venezuelan, and that as a result, on
founding the different republics that today make up this continent, their purpose was to liberate a new world so that a new
man would be born; not a citizen of Chile or of Peru, but a
citizen of America, whose race, social class, or origin would
not characterize him."[6] According to Caballero Calderón, this
type of man appears in Simón Bolívar, José de San Martín,
and José de Paula Santander. In a way they anticipated the
existence of the "South American," who is the person who not
only respects Spanish tradition and looks to Europe, but also
has his feet well rooted in America. Recalling Andrés Bello
and also Emerson, Caballero Calderón wrote: "It is not to
Europe we need to look if we aspire to create a new world
for a new man, but to ourselves." Caballero Calderón, who
has lived in Europe and has traveled and knows it extensively, knows that the "South American" does not reaffirm

or establish his personality by just denying his origin or heritage. "What characterizes the birth of a culture or a new human type is recognition of the fact that problems have begun to present themselves in another manner, or that they have ceased to present themselves because they are no longer of interest or are other problems." Fundamentally what he detests is affectation, "the intellectual make-up." He demands authenticity and detests hypocrisy.

Faithful to the idea that "man is not a dialogue but a monologue," he stated in *Latinoamérica, un mundo por hacer*: ". . . our vast Latin American world is an amorphous conglomeration of nations that are only half-nations, divided among themselves by the ruling classes that ordinarily are dull and lack ambition and historical perspective."[7]

Although Caballero Calderón belongs to a family of Spanish heritage, ruined financially while it was trying to extend Western culture to the remote regions of Colombia, he understands clearly that America is a symbiosis of cultures, of antagonisms, of aspirations. His love for the common man and for the strong traditions which exalt his country are reflected in the previously mentioned *Tipacoque* in which, according to Antonio Curcio Altamar, he reminds one of "the intellectual passion of Unamuno for the farmer and the plot of land."[8] In *Tipacoque* and in *Diario de Tipacoque* Caballero Calderón reveals his love for his country, his redemptive longings, and his perfect command of the Spanish language.

And a man preoccupied with the future of his country cannot avoid anxiety in face of the fratricidal wars that covered Colombia with blood for more than ten years. Under the tyrannical governments of Mariano Ospina Pérez (1946–1950) and of Laureano Gómez (1950–1953) violence overran Colombia. Never will one be able to know with certainty how many Colombians died from the fateful day of April 9, 1948, until the latter part of the 1950's. The po-

litical perception of Alberto Lleras Camargo saved the country from greater dangers, and his presidential administration
(1958–1963) served as a model for Valencia and Lleras Re-
strepo. In 1949 Caballero Calderón wrote in *Cartas colombianas*: "Violence is razing the fields of Colombia, poisoning
the air of the Andean highlands, and converting rural life into
a struggle without hope."[9] Nevertheless, he never lost faith in
his countrymen, "*pueblo bueno y heroico.*"

In *El Cristo de espaldas* Caballero Calderón grasps the
psychology of a small town in the midst of violence. Published
for the first time in Argentina, the novel was out of print in a
month. The second and third editions followed, and they, too,
went out of print very soon. Many Latin Americans saw themselves portrayed in *El Cristo de espaldas*. They saw in it their
own community, their own social conditions. The events
could have taken place in Peru or in Ecuador.

The protagonist is a young priest. The author shows to what
extent hatred, resentment, and mistrust are able to nullify the
peaceful and spiritual efforts of a man of deep and sincere
religious vocation. The priest, encouraged by the conviction
that the best way to serve God is to be "a rustic guardian of
poor devils," does not want to go to any large city, but rather
to immerse himself "in the melancholy purgatory of a poor
parish." An old and skeptical bishop warns him: "May God
spare you from a slow purgatory."[10]

In essence, the novel narrates the personal sacrifice of a
Christian of good faith, devoted to the idea that in spite of
ancestral hatred it is possible to establish currents of love and
understanding among men and to cause compassion to prevail. The plot of the novel unfolds in a period of five days. On
the morning following his arrival, the priest finds himself
caught in a whirlpool of small-town passions. Anacleto, son of
Don Roque, runs to the priest to seek his protection. His
father has been assassinated, and he fears the community's

wrath because he believes that they may accuse him of being the murderer. Anacarsis, his half brother and the favorite son of his father, is determined to destroy him. The two have grown up hating each other, spurred by the ill feelings of their relatives. After an absence of three years, Anacleto returns at the age of twenty-one to claim his mother's inheritance, which Don Roque has denied him on the basis that he had not reached his majority. Anacleto's presence in the community is also a challenge to the high position that Anacarsis has attained through the protection of his father. On learning of Don Roque's violent death and of the accusations against Anacleto, the priest decides to offer Anacleto personal protection and spiritual aid. All this serves as background for dialogues, political discussions, frustrations, and scenes of frank crudeness. It also serves to emphasize the religious sentiments of a priest determined to save his "flock." He realizes that salvation can be attained only through the compassion and protection of the Almighty. "Oh Lord, do not forsake us!" he cries out in desperation on one occasion while protecting Anacleto.[11]

Caballero Calderón, using the plot of a detective novel, criticizes a society corrupt with vice, violence, and contempt. He portrays the efforts of a young cleric (who defies and disobeys the old priests possessed by abulia) for social reform, in a situation characteristic of certain regions of Spanish America. The theme, in reality, is not new in the literature of the Spanish language. Pérez Galdós in *Doña Perfecta* and Tomás Carrasquilla in *El Padre Casafus*, for example, deal with similar themes. The new elements from Caballero Calderón—his real contributions—are the pathos, the temperate use of the language, the authentic description of the Spanish American state of affairs, the moral message, the opposition to indifference, abuse, and graft. The priest, struggling with the mandates of his conscience and the cruelty of his adversaries, prefers to defend the idea that God must prevail. And when as father-confessor he learns directly from the dying "Caricortao" who the real assassin is, he keeps the secret in accord with his oath as a priest. Nevertheless, all is in vain: he means nothing to his "flock," and Anacleto is the victim of the community's wrath. Nor does the Bishop understand his mission, for he finally writes to Anacleto scornfully: "Pretend, my son, that Christ has turned his back." To which the young priest replies mentally: "Father, forgive them, for they know not what they do!"[12]

Caballero Calderón is representative, as we have said, of those novelists who are preoccupied with their country and with the political future of America. But he is not alone. Even in those novels of marked psychological tenor or in which new techniques are being tried, social concerns predominate. Spanish America, through her restlessness, her contrasts, her infamies, and her great moments (whether expressed in *Los pasos perdidos* of Alejo Carpentier or in *El Señor Presidente* of Miguel Angel Asturias) allows us to perceive her passionate and volcanic life. And the novelist depicts these scenes with lifelike intensity and passion.

Notes

[1] Jorge Mañach, "Gabriela: alma y tierra," *Revista Hispánica Moderna*, Vol. 3 (1936–37), p. 109.

[2] John Oliver Killens, *The New York Times Magazine*, June 7, 1964, p. 37, in an article on Negro culture.

[3] Roger Caillois, "Les thèmes fondamentaux de J. L. Borges," *L'Herne: J. L. Borges*, ed. by Dominique de Roux and Jean de Milleret (Paris, 1964), p. 211.

[4] Jorges Luis Borges, "Composición escrita en un ejemplar de la gesta de Bowulf [*sic*]," in *Antología Personal* (Buenos Aires, 1961), p. 195.

[5] Juan Lozano y Lozano, "Prólogo," in Eduardo Caballero Calderón, *Obras*, 3 vols. (Medellín, Colombia, 1963), Vol. 1, p. ix.

[6] Eduardo Caballero Calderón, *Suramérica, tierra del hombre* (Medellín, Colombia, 1944), p. 247.

[7] Eduardo Caballero Calderón, *Latinoamérica, un mundo por hacer,* in *Obras,* Vol. 2, p. 18.

[8] Antonio Curcio Altamar, *Evolución de la novela en Colombia* (Bogotá, 1957), p. 255.

[9] Caballero Calderón, "Con posdata," *Cartas Colombianas,* in *Obras,* Vol. 2, p. 225.

[10] Eduardo Caballero Calderón, *El Cristo de espaldas,* 2nd ed. (Buenos Aires, 1952), p. 23.

[11] Caballero Calderón, *El Cristo de espaldas,* p. 72.

[12] Caballero Calderón, *El Cristo de espaldas,* p. 165.

ARTISTS AND WRITERS

IN

THE EVOLUTION OF LATIN AMERICA

Art and Life in Mexico and Brazil

Francisco Monterde

Art and Life in Mexico

THE WORDS ART AND LIFE are used together here because today in Mexico they are frequently mingled and confused as much as or more than in any other country. ART. LIFE. It is not easy to separate one from the other, and to speak of Mexican art apart from Mexican life.

I shall begin by telling you that Mexico is a land of sudden changes, surprises, and contrasts, as already pointed out by many. It is sufficient to read the works of such a famous traveler as Alexander von Humboldt, or an inquisitive and attentive one like Madame Calderón de la Barca, to have an idea of these contrasts.

The first observation made by the traveler is the great difference which exists in Mexico—and in the greater part of Hispanic America, perhaps—between the country and the city, as if they were different worlds, or two aspects of different periods.

A South American thinker, the versatile Domingo F. Sarmiento, in whose work *Facundo: Civilización y Barbarie* the ideas of Bolívar, Buckle, and Spencer appear side by side, speaks of the struggle between the country and the city—of warring brothers of his day in his country. What he says about Argentina may be applied to other republics, for in the same social mediums the problems are similar, the only difference being one of time. In some countries events developed rapidly, in others slowly.

This may serve also to explain the reason for establishing the difference between, and speaking separately of, life and art in the city and life and art among the people of the country—that is to say, the art of the city and the popular arts.

To judge by testimony of the past, revealed by the study of archeology, this conflict has always existed in the land formerly called Anáhuac.

Scattered through its vast territory are found remains of vanished civilizations. Each nucleus of a culture left vestiges that are more or less artistic, according to the degree of culture achieved. The Temple of Quetzalcóatl at Teotihuacán presents architectural details belonging to civilizations of different epochs. Archeologists have described these constructions, and they reveal the tragedy of a peaceful people, advanced in the arts, who were conquered by another, inferior in everything except the art of warfare.

The sojourn of that cultured people—the Toltecs—is marked by buildings whose ruins show details of architecture, sculpture, and painting that reveal, in part, their secrets: the secrets of a superior religion whose worship was not one of bloody sacrifices, as was that of those who followed it.

No doubt the minor arts of the Indians, who produced the beautiful examples kept in the museums, are due also in large part to that people. In ceramic art they produced vases perfect in form and beautifully decorated. The frets of their textiles were in no way inferior to the ornamentation in the friezes of their monuments.

The warlike tribe that later took possession of the valley took advantage of the solidity of the Toltec constructions to build upon them their own temples, using the foundations for new pyramids, which lack the original primitive decoration. The Aztecs learned also.

They learned to cover with blue stone mosaic work the polished surfaces of skulls and masks, and laboriously to make mosaics from the luxurious feathers of the humming bird, brought them as tribute from the region of Michoacán. The dominion of Atzcapotzalco was famous for its gold workers; the gold that Moctezuma received as gifts from his vassals was transformed into delicate jewelry, which the Spanish conquerors, already accustomed to the luxury of Italy, found marvelous.

In spite of this, the oppression of the Aztecs weighed like a heavy yoke upon the neighboring communities and prepared the way for Spanish domination. In the codices, or primitive documents, we find dark hieroglyphic representations of human footprints marking the way of emigration. These traces seem to tell us of the terror of those pursued, who left behind them their treasures of art and of their learning to be picked up by their pursuers.

The carved stones in Xochicalco, Mitla, Uxmal, and Chichén Itzá speak of the life before the coming of Cortés; in a more gentle tongue the legends which find no place in history tell us of their complicated theory of God; and likewise the poems, which we regard even today as hymns, and in which I see the dialogue of an embryonic theatre.

The artistic impulse was not interrupted by the arrival of the Spanish conquerors. When the bewilderment of the new warfare had passed, the Indians of Amantla again busied themselves with their feather mosaics, which they studied in a static ecstasy. At times they studied an entire day without adding a new feather, in doubt as to which one of the great variety of colors suited best.

The *Tlacuilos* continued painting frescos, and the sculptors, now using marvelous new tools brought by the Spaniards, kept on carving stones. But there was one great difference: both the painter and the sculptor had to replace the idolatrous figures with the image of the new God. Their ideas of Deity, little by little, became confused with Spanish legends and tales of miracles, and the first words spoken by the white men began to appear in their primitive documents.

Before the arrival of the Spaniards, the works of art served to embellish the rites of idol worship. Afterwards, they served to adorn the temples and the palaces of the new lords.

The centres of artistic production, which formerly were to be found around the palaces, were gradually moved, and set up in the vicinity of churches and monasteries.

The ships which brought officials and trade goods, arrived from time to time at the shores of New Spain, bringing new objects, many of them from the Orient, to influence Mexican ornamentation.

Meanwhile, in the capital, the first painters of the old world filled enormous canvasses with images and symbols to decorate the church walls, while the Indians patiently carved the altars; and missionaries like Vasco de Quiroga created new centres of arts and crafts.

Don Vasco, in Michoacán, founded an organization of craftsmen who, today, are still giving their products to the world. So thorough was the instruction that it has survived the ages and still continues.

Others, with less organization, encouraged the local industries, so that places like Oaxaca, Jalisco, and Guanajuato might produce their own ceramics, making use of the local clay and minerals. In Amozoc were made exquisite inlays of silver on iron, similar to the gold on iron made in Éibar, Spain, and the Mexican workmanship was in no way inferior to the Spanish.

The talavera ware of Puebla is said to rival in New Spain the Talavera de la Reina pottery which is famous in the Spanish peninsula; and in the north of the country, as well as in the extreme south, silk, linen, and wool are all used to create unique textiles.

In Mexico, life followed its course, but with a new rhythm

in which the slowness of the Indian was quickened by the stimulus of the Spaniard. Now we have two distinct social mediums, each with different manifestations of art.

The city was becoming enriched with mansions of carved stone, into which the Spanish architect introduced strong motifs, and the Indian sculptor, with the sure instinct of Indian ancestry for decorative details, added the charm that became the characteristic stamp of colonial architecture, religious as well as civil.

The temples of the city have images and altars of gold, and choir lofts created by woodcarvers and masters of inlaid work. Private houses exhibit, as a touch of luxury, their carved doors with coats of arms of the Spanish nobility, their iron railings, and their fountains where the water falls musically into a flower-bordered mirror.

The country has only the humble *jacal*, with its straw roof; but within these huts, in the midst of poverty, objects are made which adorn the homes of the wealthy. The women tirelessly rub beautiful colored gourds, giving them a polish similar to that of Oriental lacquerware. The men weave palm leaves or transfer to cloth a garden spot or the beauty of a rainbow.

At this point we begin to see the difference between the art cultivated in the city and that which was born and developed freely in the country.

In the creations of the craftsmen of New Spain during the reign of the viceroys, one sees the perfect repose in which they were conceived and carried out. We see the influence of the Orient, coming from the objects which were brought by the so-called *Nao de China* (Ship from Manila). The artists, protected by the monasteries and supported by the rich mineowners, such as, for example, Don José de la Borda, worked absolutely free from material worries and gave themselves spiritually to their creative work, which, as Jesús

Acevedo remarks, can only be compared with the majestic works that have come from the hands of the craftsmen in India and old China.

However, the colonial art, in spite of its lofty theme and its merits, did not escape certain limitations. In subject matter it was almost always mystic and at times aristocratic; only a few popular works have escaped this tendency, and these objects have ever since been popular with the Creoles for their personal adornment or for the decoration of their dwellings.

The country people, exploited by the overlord in order to satiate the appetites of the city and of the Spanish fatherland, were the ones who, by their constancy, brought a triumphant conclusion to Mexico's struggle for independence; and it was they who laid the foundations for the Republic after the attempt to perpetuate a European style of monarchy on the North American continent, which is known in Mexican history by the name of the Second Empire.

The Independence was anticipated in the writings of José Joaquín Fernández de Lizardi (El Pensador Mexicano), the initiator of the real national literature. The literary production of three centuries of Spanish domination had been no more than a pale reflection of the literature of Spain, and it is saved from oblivion only by two outstanding figures—the great dramatist Juan Ruiz de Alarcón and the great poetess Sor Juana Inés de la Cruz. Both have been comprehensively studied by our scholars, who have done so much to make known those celebrated figures of Mexican literature.

The Pensador Mexicano—creator of the Mexican novel, publisher and moralist and versatile author of many works—is somewhat different from his predecessors but equally worthy of attention and study, for he created a new artistic style, in which the people appear both as the point of departure and the subject. Even though Fernández de Lizardi was born and lived in the city most of his life, his ideology, intention, and style are nearer to the popular literature.

During the past century and up to the present moment, literary art has been oscillating continuously between the city and the country, between our own native characteristics and those from abroad; Ricardo Rojas has called these "Indianism and Exotism," the extreme points between which the soul of the Hispanic American people moves without having, as yet, found its fixed place.

In Mexico, as in other countries, literature is alternately erudite and popular. Today writers prefer topics dealing with the workman and the country people, rather than with the exotic and aristocratic subjects dealt with in previous times. The last generations have given writers the theme for novels and short stories in which appears the soul of a people in the process of formation—the soul of a people struggling to define its own personality and to adjust each of its parts, as in an unsolved puzzle.

The poets, after reechoing the epic poetry of Spain, followed on the waves of French poetry: the Romantic, Parnassian, and Symbolist. It was Ramón López Velarde who made us turn our eyes toward ourselves. Since that time, in literature the city has looked with interest at things pertaining to the country.

The real beginning of the artistic renaissance in Mexico may be said to be 1915. Architecture, sculpture, painting, music, literature, and the minor arts, dormant for nearly a century because of political and military disturbances, awakened simultaneously.

The impulse to restore the interrupted artistic tradition was reborn in the city. José Clemente Orozco was the initiator who, like Daumier in France, observed and castigated the vices of a depraved society. Diego Rivera and his followers covered walls with themes inspired by the proletarian vic-

tories and glorified the humble country worker, thereby re-
newing the fresco painting previously employed only in
church ornamentation.

From the city also came the impulse that was to rejuvenate
—excessively at times—the colonial architecture of gray stone
and *tezontle* (red stone) as well as the minor arts used in
exterior and interior decoration. To this task we writers have
contributed by demanding that architectural monuments be
respected and ennobled.

On the other hand, in order to bring about a musical renaissance, composers from the city had to go to the country in
search of songs and native melodies, repeated today by singers
who formerly sang the imported and borrowed music of
foreign romances.

Dramatic art is slowly struggling to assert itself with plays
in which the life of the city and the country are united and
fused in anticipation of a future well-being.

It would be useless to attempt to speak to you in detail
about the renaissance of Mexican art, which coincided with
the reorganizations born after our frequent upheavals. Doctor
Atl, apostle of the popular arts, collected his efforts and observations in a fine book a complete exposition of our industrial art, which is waiting to be organized on a cooperative
basis to permit an equal sharing of the profits from it.

Periodically the people of the country send to popular fairs
in the capital and other cities their handicraft, which almost
always preserves its typical features. The *puestos* (small curio
shops and stands) which were formerly set up around the city
park, beautified by the viceroy Luis de Velasco, Senior, are
still veritable expositions of handicraft; the materials used are
most varied, and in nearly every case the articles displayed
seem far superior to what one would expect of artisans of such
limited intellectual and material resources.

As I see the problem, except in isolated cases which the

future may well rectify, art in Mexico is now taking a course parallel to life, from which in other times it had remained separate. Thus it approaches more and more the ancient ideal, which was to produce great works with national but also universal characteristics.

My personal hope is that someday Mexico may attain this ideal, which is seldom reached except when city and country march along in the same rhythm—when there is harmony between man and nature, and within men themselves.

Lester C. Walker, Jr.

The Revolution of 1910 as Reflected
in Mexican Art

THE REFLECTION of the 1910 Revolution in Mexican art
is popularly found in the outburst of mural painting produced
during the period 1920–1925, especially in works by Rivera,
Orozco, and Siqueiros. The themes are, first, a glorification
of the military and social aspects of the Revolutionary
struggle, and, second, a celebration of those cultural characteristics that are uniquely Mexican and Indian. The devices
often caricature contrary aspects such as the Conquest,
Colonialism, the Church, Foreign Intervention (including
Yankee Imperialism), and unpopular dictators.

Since most persons with a background in Mexican art already know the Ministry of Education frescos by Rivera, or
those on the stairway of the National Palace, which present
heavy-handed propaganda produced some years after the
initial phases of the Revolution, it is unnecessary to discuss
them here. My purpose will be to note some events from the
earlier premural period. The genesis of a few of the artists
who later produced the frescos will be scanned to search for
formative factors in their work, so that we will be able to
evaluate more accurately the florescence between 1920 and
1925.

As one who is more accustomed to exploring a work of art
than a political-social system, I find the 1910 Revolutionary
scene in Mexico to be infinitely confusing. The one thing that

seems to make 1910 stand out, beyond the fact that it was the 100th anniversary of the *Grito de Dolores,* is that the fall of Díaz indicated the emergence of the forces that finally returned Mexico to the Mexicans. These forces, more psychological than political, were hampered by a ghastly national dogfight until the constructive aspects of the Revolution, extending over many years, began to draw the nation together. It is the glorification of the unique Indian and Mexican cultural factors that provided the potential of the self-realizing national destiny upon which Mexico is successfully building today. That art was consciously employed toward this goal is significant. Reference to a few aspects of this emergence will follow.

At the beginning of the 20th century, Mexico, after almost three centuries of Spanish Colonialism and a century of confused "Independence," found its masses despised and impoverished, its Indian culture subordinated, its national resources exploited for the benefit of the few, and its own national identity a question mark. Mexico's art was, likewise, foreign. The Royal Academy of Fine Arts of San Carlos was founded in 1785 by its first director, Jerónimo Antonio Gil, master engraver to the Spanish King, who was originally sent to Mexico in 1778 to supervise "the art standards and metal casting craft of its mint."[1] The San Carlos Academy generally determined official Mexican art, which was often neglected, as attested by Fanny Calderón de la Barca's observation in 1840: "The present disorder and abandoned state of the building, the nonexistence of these excellent classes of sculpture and painting, and, above all, the low state of the fine arts in Mexico at the present day, are among the sad proofs, if any were wanting, of the melancholy effects produced by years of civil war and unsettled government."[2]

The national show of economic stability by Mexico under Porfirio Díaz brought official support for San Carlos, which was accented for the 1910 Centennial. The new Italian Baroque Revival Palacio de Bellas Artes and the nearby Renaissance Revival Post Office illustrate the standards. Thirty-five thousand pesos were set aside for a display of *Spanish art*, and a special building was constructed for the purpose. More indicative of impending changes in the orientation of art in Mexico was the "Show of Works of National Art," squeezed into the halls of San Carlos on a budget of three thousand pesos. This exhibit was somewhat at odds with the usual official stance of the institution, which had drawn its leaders and its whole orientation from Europe.

Occasionally there was talk of a National Art, and unrest with the foreign domination bubbled through the official art front, as it did through the political scene. The evidence is documented by a declaration found in the San Carlos archives for 1911: "By general agreement and unanimous vote none should attend the Anatomy class until its teacher resigns. . . . Long live Democracy! Down with the *científicos* in this school. Free suffrage. Liberty and Constitution. Mexico, July 15 of the year of Freedoms."[3]

The political revolutionary state of mind was thus reflected in Mexico's art center. A student strike at San Carlos, indicated in the above declaration, smouldered through the unfulfilled hope of the Madero period, when the locked-out students went to the public parks to sketch, until Ramos Martínez came to be director in 1913. Martínez instituted the first open-air art school at Santa Anita, taking his cue from the students' outdoor sketching while on strike. This "Barbizon" approach served as a prototype for the open-air schools of Vasconcelos a decade later. A self-conscious nationalism in art was appearing, to be later fostered by publications such as Dr. Atl's *Las artes populares en México*, in which he wrote: "Si quisiera concretarse el juicio sobre las artes populares en México en sus relaciones etnológicas con las artes de otros países podría decirse: México ocupa en el mundo el tercer lugar entre los pueblos productores de artes manuales—el segundo lugar corresponde al Japón y el primero a China."⁴

Indian art, from pre-Columbian times to modern times was eventually to emerge into the realm of respectability.

Dr. Atl, designer of the Tiffany curtain in Bellas Artes, was of primary importance as a radical catalyst for art of the Revolution in Mexico. He discarded his real name, Gerardo Murillo, because of its similarity to that of the 17th century Spanish religious painter, and adopted *Atl* from an Indian word as a badge of honor. This action was symptomatic of forces at work. Those seeking evidence of indigenous bases in Mexican art found it in other places also.

José María Velasco is credited with the real discovery of Mexican landscape. His great panoramas, with their consciousness of the tremendous space that is the Mexican countryside, brought to the people a new awareness of the land and to Mexico's developing artists, an uncommonly advanced understanding of new problems in art. In 1903, Diego Rivera as a student at San Carlos acquired his basic understanding of space from Velasco. This was before Rivera went to Europe to participate successfully as a cubist painter along with the creators of that significant approach to modern abstraction. Jean Charlot points out: "Velasco's solid teachings spared Rivera the stage of impressionism fashionable at that date in progressive European art schools. Instead, his severely logical approach to optical problems prepared the adolescent for the further rationalizations of cubism."⁵

Velasco's honest landscapes do not shout chauvinism, but they search clearly, longingly, and lovingly through all the reaches of the amazing land of Mexico, and make apology to no one. Their excellence was recognized by an Award of Merit at the 1876 Centennial in Philadelphia, and the critic José Martí, writing in *Revista Universal*, October 14, 1876, said in reference to this success: "To say that Mexican paint-

ing has no future . . . may be true in Mexico, where rich men
lack equally in artistic knowledge, patriotic love, and good
taste. But Mexican painting has a great future outside Mexico."[6]

Less sophisticated bases for genuine Mexican painting
were found in the folk art-pulquería paintings of each little
village—those anecdotal delineations of common events, legends, and earthy humor formerly regarded as beneath proper
consideration as *Art*. Closely related to the pulquería paintings were the popular engravings, caricatures, often executed
in wryly bitter humor, of the daily tragedies that had to be
shrugged off by the Indian in order to exist. The most illustrious and often cited master in this media was José Guadalupe Posada, who came to Mexico City in 1887 to work for
the publishing house of Antonio Vanegas Arroyo, where, before his death in 1913, his career and influence overlapped the
most important Revolutionary artists.

Posada's raw macabre humor gave an outlet for the incredible frustrations of so many Mexicans and provided a sharp,
satiric insight into injustices and imbalances underneath the
Porfirian cover. The sensational publications of Vanegas Arroyo, illustrated by Posada, exercised a morbid fascination for
youngsters. Orozco in his *Autobiography* tells of the hours
spent watching the engraver work. A similar story is told of
Rivera, who later acknowledged Posada by comparing him
to Goya and Callot.

Often much is made in extolling the virtues of a *new* movement by emphasizing how bad the *old* was and what rebellious struggles were necessary in order to see things in their
proper light. This is part of the recurrent cycle of new life
determining its own destiny. Humans are ambivalent figures
who adjust their responses to the moment and to that with
which they feel familiar. Orozco was obviously fascinated by
the ingratiating propaganda of Dr. Atl, who, while conducting
night classes at San Carlos, did much to subvert the strict

discipline of the Academy by revolutionary tactics. Orozco eventually followed Dr. Atl into active participation in the Revolution; yet in a more conservative view Orozco wrote: "The cancer of Bohemianism attacked young painters, destroying will power, talent, and lives; this was the Bohemianism we recognize in the symptoms of lank locks, laziness, filth, alcohol, and various diseases."[7]

Orozco seems to have regarded his participation in the student strikes at San Carlos as a quite natural activity, and notes: "Rebellious ideas went on fermenting in the young painters of 1910, greatly stimulated by the general state of political disorder throughout the country."[8]

The personal turmoil of the artists at San Carlos, as that of the people of Mexico, was ready to boil through the surface, for the frustrated heat of years had built up to such a degree that there was no possibility of evading the scalding catharsis. For a short time San Carlos Academy wooed its dissident student strikers with visions of French landscape pleasantries in the open-air school in Santa Anita called, too obviously, *Barbizon*. Orozco preferred ". . . the pestilent shadows of closed rooms, and instead of the Indian male, drunken ladies and gentlemen."[9] He claims that he played no part in the Revolution, specifically the period up to 1917, referring to it as "the gayest and most diverting of carnivals."[10] During those early days he describes the capital: "By night the city was fantastic. Countless haunts of dissipation were crowded with women of easy morals and officers from Huerta's army. . . . One of the most frequented spots in Huertist times was the Teatro María Guerrero. . . . The audience was utterly hybrid; the filthiest scum of the city mixed with intellectuals and artists, with army officers, bureaucrats, politicians, and even secretaries of state. They conducted themselves worse than at bullfights."[11]

During the Madero period Orozco had a position as cari-

caturist for an opposition newspaper. He wrote of the experience: "I might equally well have gone to work for a government paper instead of the opposition, and in that case the
scapegoats would have been on the other side. No artist has,
or ever has had, political convictions of any sort. Those who
profess to have them are not artists."[12] Yet he goes on, "The
Madero episode, a half-revolution, was sheer confusion and
senselessness. Except for this everything remained what it had
always been."

The heat from the caldron of war often brings the scum to
the surface. Other people must be tempered from the vacillating malleability of their indeterminate mass into the hard,
sharp steel that can survive such a trial. That tempering was
ahead of Orozco and was to be reflected in the horrid, biting
Goyaesque caricatures of Revolutionary dissolution to be seen
in Orozco's wartime cartoons and later paintings.

The socialist artist and propagandist, Dr. Atl, came back
from European intrigues and anti-Huerta activities in time to
sway his art-student followers from Villa to Carranza. Then,
in the impending descent of Villa on Mexico City, he loaded
artists, writers, and printing equipment on the last train for
Orizaba, where churches were taken over and the Revolutionary newspaper *La Vanguardia* established. Dr. Atl was
editor in chief and Clemente Orozco caricaturist. The carefree cynicism Orozco expressed in the Madero period continued, temporarily. He wrote: "Life in Orizaba was of the
most agreeable and entertaining character. We worked en-
thusiastically. The town was lively. There was music on all
sides, . . . and I did handbills and furious anticlerical caricatures."[13] But later he wrote: "But the world was torn apart
around us. Troop convoys passed on their way to slaughter.
Trains were blown up. In the portals of the churches wretched
Zapatista peasants, who had fallen prisoners to the Carrancis-
tas, were summarily shot down."[14]

The carnival was over. The Revolution continued its horrible course in an upside-down existence that made no sense. Orozco was saved from actual fighting because of the loss of one hand in an early accident. In 1917 we find him leaving for the United States, since he did not find his own distraught country very receptive to art. Doubtless he had much upon which to reflect before the opportunity came, some years later, to paint great murals. And then, when he was at his best, Orozco painted as a violently indignant artist, his works full of the agitation, horror, degradation, and frustrated antagonisms of a people at war with themselves. He had seen it. The case with Rivera was somewhat different. Rivera, three years younger than Orozco, also found instruction in the engravings of Posada. But, while Orozco translated the open-faced garishness of Posada into expositions of wartime decadence, Rivera produced technically competent theoretical studies in avant-garde European art or fluent and charming observations of facets of his own country. It was not until long after the bitter Revolutionary fighting, which he did not personally experience, that Rivera turned increasingly to shrill photomontagelike pastiches such as that of the stairway of the National Palace. This was commissioned in 1929, after a period in Russia in 1927 and 1928.[15] It is much like an arranged series of newsphotos. The paintings of the Revolutionary fighting, in the Patio of Festivals of the Ministry of Education, are likewise strongly reflective of the European, not the Mexican, Revolution. It is when Rivera paints something with which he is sympathetically emotionally involved from first-hand experience that he is at his best, such as in the symbolic figures of the Agricultural School at Chapingo, painted when his life was deeply enmeshed with that of Lupe Marín. He also seems to have been able to establish a sympathetic harmony with syntheses of aspects of Mexico, as in the frescos of the Palace of Cortés at Cuernavaca. It is then that, to me, he seems truly to reflect Mexico. But his paintings of scenes of the Mexican Revolution are basically European. They could hardly be otherwise.

Rivera left San Carlos Academy in 1902 when he was sixteen. Five years later he gained government support for study in Europe. After three years in Spain he moved on to Paris. Europe was preparing for an even more efficient effort at self-destruction in impending World War I than Mexico's in its Revolution. Having returned home only for a successful exhibition in the twilight of Porfirianism during the Centennial, Rivera, who had been in Paris, could know his country's Revolution only abstractly. Actually he was closer to the conflict of theoretical ideologies in Europe than to the stench of the Mexican battlefields or its hordes of roving Zapatistas. During the period of 1913 he is described as restlessly traveling, reading, and seeking answers to his unrest. One of the influential books he read was Karl Marx's *Das Capital.*

Rivera experienced physical hardships in the decade 1911–1921 in Paris, where he was an active member of the avant-garde art circles and a successful cubist painter. His associations ran strongly toward the persons displaced by the European war, and he had a manifest sympathy for the Russian Revolution, to which he was closer than to that of his own country. Yet, Rivera's omnipresent frescos probably will, in the irony of historical distortion, come to be the images known to future generations as the Mexican Revolution. I see them more as an extension of the Communist struggle.

The third member of the Mexican triumvirate of Revolutionary painters, David Alfaro Siqueiros is less well known in the United States than Rivera or Orozco, is less easy to discuss, and is the only one of the three major Revolutionary painters still living. Younger than the other two, he nevertheless as a very young student of fifteen participated in the San Carlos student strike of 1911, of which he said: "All our modern painting movement stems from this act of pedagogical political rebellion. It was this action, however infantile, that established our first contact with the living problems of Mexico and the Mexican people."[16]

Siqueiros went with Dr. Atl and Orozco to Orizaba and then to the Constitutional Army, where he became a lieutenant. In 1914 he became a member of the staff of General Manuel M. Diéguez, foe of Villa. In 1919 Siqueiros received a military and diplomatic assignment to Paris. There he was in close communication with Rivera and European radicals, through whom his revolutionary ideology was intensified. In May 1921 from Barcelona Siqueiros published his *Manifesto a los Plásticos de América* in *Vida Americana*, over which he had recently gained control. The manifesto was a complex of calls to the future and a reflection of the influences that had shaken European painting during the two previous decades. It included the following statement: "An understanding of the admirable human content of 'Negro Art' and of 'primitive art' in general has oriented the plastic arts toward a clarity and depth lost for four centuries in an underbrush of indecisions; as regards ourselves, we must come closer to the works of the ancient settlers of our vales, Indian painters and sculptors (Mayan, Aztec, Inca, etc., etc.). . . . Let us borrow their synthetic energy, but let us avoid lamentable archaeological reconstructions so fashionable among us, 'Indianism,' 'Primitivism,' 'Americanism.' "[17]

At the time this manifesto appeared, the mural program in Mexico was being initiated. Obregon became president in 1920. José Vasconcelos, who had been Minister of Education a short time under Eulalio Gutiérrez and was subsequently stranded in exile in the United States from 1915 to 1920, returned. In lieu of the Ministry of Education post, which had been abolished under Carranza, Vasconcelos was made rector of the University and entered a vigorous campaign to solicit support for reestablishment of the Ministry of Education.

Vasconcelos, a lawyer and an amazingly agile Revolutionary official when physical survival was literally a day-to-day affair, was also a philosopher with an esthetic ideal for his educational program. Esthetic philosophy and political survival were expeditiously joined by the theme of nationalism in art as a means to justify the expense that would be involved, and to recognize and make use of one of the underlying psychological drives of the Revolution—the realization of a national and personal identity and integrity. Indian Mexico and Hispanic Mexico have had strong basic affinities for art, although the outward manifestations might differ. Vasconcelos took musicians, poets, and artists on his campaign tour to develop support for his program. He dates the Mexican painting renaissance from this trip in 1920.[18]

Although the idea of mural painting for the people had been born, the initial stages were chaotic. Roberto Montenegro, who had gone on Vasconcelos' political campaign, had a position of priority and was given walls, upon which to paint the first government sponsored murals of the Mexican painting renaissance, in the hastily obtained old convent of San Pedro and San Pablo in Mexico City. The result, an inconsequential decorative work, was hardly reflective of the intense drama needed to elicit popular support for the program.

A small amount of public money for *Art* in a democratic nation is much less readily justifiable by politicians than huge sums for arms. Vasconcelos was rapidly forced to stronger nationalistic emphases in order to meet the critics, and he turned to the talents of scattered Mexican artists of dramatic ability, who began returning from their foreign travels. The convent adjoining San Pedro and San Pablo was to be reconstructed as an educational center, an annex to the Preparatory School, and the formerly flamboyant Dr. Atl was to be ap-

pointed to work on the decorations. Orozco came back from
the United States, Rivera and Siqueiros from Europe, along
with many others long out of their country. Atl and Rivera
immediately launched into noisy conflict. Favored Montenegro painted the first true fresco in the annex; it was subsequently damaged by opposing students, and punishments
were invoked for the desecration. A well-publicized hassle en-
sued.

The full course of the Revolution was not yet run, but the
direction of its art work was already established. I will conclude with a quotation from Orozco: "By 1922, when the
Revolution had produced a strong, prosperous government, it
was possible for us to suggest doing murals in keeping with
the ideas of 1910, which had already evolved in the direction
of social interests."[19]

Notes

[1] Jean Charlot, *Mexican Art and the Academy of San Carlos, 1785–1915*
(Austin, 1962), p. 20.

[2] Madame Fanny Calderon de la Barca, *Life in Mexico, During a Resi-
dence of Two Years in That Country* (London, 1843), p. 103.

[3] Jean Charlot, *The Mexican Mural Renaissance, 1920–1925* (New Haven
and London, 1963), p. 44.

[4] "If one would like to make a more precise judgment about popular arts
in Mexico in its ethnological relations with arts in other countries, it could
be said that Mexico occupies third place in the world among the countries
that produce manual arts; second place is held by Japan; China is first." Dr.
Atl, *Las Artes Populares en México*, Vol. 1 (México, 1923), p. 17.

[5] Charlot, *Mexican Art and the Academy of San Carlos, 1785–1915*, p. 142.

[6] Charlot, *The Mexican Mural Renaissance, 1920–1925*, p. 56.

[7] José Clemente Orozco, *An Autobiography*, translated by Robert C.
Stephenson (Austin, 1962), p. 26.

[8] Orozco, *An Autobiography*, p. 30.

[9] Orozco, *An Autobiography*, p. 40.

[10] *Orozco, An Autobiography*, p. 40.

[11] Orozco, *An Autobiography*, pp. 42–45.

[12] Orozco, *An Autobiography*, p. 30.

[13] Orozco, *An Autobiography*, p. 53.

[14] Orozco, *An Autobiography*, p. 54.

[15] Emily Edwards, *Painted Walls of Mexico* (Austin and London, 1966), p. 204.

[16] Alma M. Reed, *The Mexican Muralists* (New York, 1960), p. 100.

[17] Charlot, *The Mexican Mural Renaissance, 1920–1925*, p. 73.

[18] Charlot, *The Mexican Mural Renaissance, 1920–1925*, p. 96.

[19] Carlos Pellicer, *et al.*, *Mural Painting of the Mexican Revolution* (México, 1960), p. 58.

Comments BY EDWARD H. MOSELEY

Professor Lester C. Walker offered several important ideas that reach far beyond the field of painting. For one thing, he demonstrated that Revolutionary artists could get along with each other no better than could Revolutionary generals and politicians. His major theme, however, seems to center on a single sentence: "Yet, Rivera's omnipresent frescos probably will, in the irony of historical distortion, come to be the images known to future generations as the Mexican Revolution." This statement is subject to challenge. I would contend that the murals of Rivera *are today* accepted as the true reflection of the great event.

Every society faces the problem of distorted history. The younger generation of the United States now views World War II as a fuzzy combination of *The Rat Patrol*, and *Hogan's Heroes*. In the case of Mexico's Revolution, the distortion has taken the form of an idealized nationalism, supported by a set of altruistic principles. Even the agonizing expressions and twisted bodies portrayed by Orozco have come to glorify events which he viewed with disgust. Perhaps those of us in the social sciences who have often referred to the works of Rivera and Siqueiros as "artistic reflections of the Revolution," might now change our statement, and say that these murals are actually "artistic distortions" of the movement.

Mário Ypiranga Monteiro

The Influence of Intellectuals
in the Evolution of Brazil

It is often said that the biggest obstacle to the evolution of Brazil in the sciences has been the inclination of the Brazilian toward arts and letters and toward living more in the realm of spiritual exploration than in the field of technological advancement, planned research, and scientific applications. This fact is easily observed today, four hundred and sixty-eight years after the discovery of Brazil.

The humanistic bent of the Brazilian does not mean that Brazil has not had men dedicated to the solution of technical-scientific problems. It is customary to say, however, that each and every Brazilian is a poet when he is nineteen—a result, perhaps, of his natural exuberance, the beauty of his environment, and his emotional heritage.

Men like Father Bartolomeu Lourenço de Gusmão and Manuel Alexandre Rodrigues Ferreira—the former being the inventor of the *aerostato* [gas balloon] and the latter a renowned naturalist—made great contributions to scientific knowledge in the colonial period and are good examples of our inventive capacity. Alberto Santos Dumont (1873–1932) in the period of the Republic revolutionized air navigation, setting Paris agog with the presentation of his various flying machines. The remarkable thing about Gusmão is that his experiments were conducted on August 7, 1709—seventy-four years before those of the Montgolfier brothers—in Lisbon, which was dominated by the Inquisition. As one might expect, the Inquisition condemned his experiments. Gusmão was a professor of mathematics at Coimbra University, and he left some unpublished works, among them a manual on air navigation.

However, Brazilians who made a contribution outside the field of arts and literature are not very well known, some merely because of lack of capacity to exploit their inventions. Poorly oriented colonialism is blamed for the slow evolution of Brazil in science and technology, and actually there were few conditions or stimuli for the creation of a technological mind. During the colonial period, Brazilians did not possess schools of higher learning with their capacity to spread culture. Only primary schools directed by priests existed in Brazil. It was after the arrival of Dom João VI in 1808 that the first schools of surgery were opened, one in Bahia and the other in Rio de Janeiro. (In that epoch the National Museum and the Botanical Garden were also founded.) There was not, therefore, an educational basis for cultural development. The few Brazilians who could—generally religious men—went to European universities, but their main tendency was towards a career in the Church. (The Church did give us excellent researchers, of the calibre of Friar Veloso, author of *Flora Fluminense*.)

The social framework, which was devoid of institutions of higher learning and in which economic policies cannot be ignored, prevented a greater national achievement and more widespread activities in the field of pure science. In contrast, artists and men of letters sprang up like mushrooms in the country because social conditions and their own natural tendency encouraged them.

Since colonial times, a nationalistic spirit has developed among men of letters, artists, and artisans, due to the realization that the existence of social inequality and injustice was the result of the poorly oriented colonial regime of the Portuguese monarchy. It was during the colonial regime that the first struggles towards political emancipation took place, along with a tendency toward independence of language. Brazilians having a European university education were influenced by the political successes generated by humanistic philosophy in Europe, and through their speeches the seeds of Brazilian separation were sown.

It cannot be said that the first separatist movements truly represented the opposition of intellectuals to the cultural conservatism of the colonial government. Apparently they were, rather, reactions against the economic and cultural policies implanted in the colony, which tended to perpetuate social injustices. On the other hand, although the Portuguese language remained as the instrument of normal communication, the more nationalistic men of letters made use of native elements to oppose the domination of that language. For example, Father José de Anchieta (1534–1597), a Jesuit, did not openly strive for equality for the Indian language with Portuguese in his bilingual theater. The trend of the times, however, was expressed in the choice of national motifs and Indian words—which were later to appear in nativist poetry. Father Anchieta was effective in the moral education of the Brazilian Indians in the region east of São Paulo by means of his theater, which used only native themes presented in both the Indian and Portuguese languages mixed with some Spanish. (Later another Jesuit, Father Antônio Vieira [1608–1697], a great preacher of the Amazon region, was to use the pulpit to stir up the natives as well as the Portuguese settlers against the colonial government, in the process almost running afoul of the Inquisition. He was the leader of the opposition to Negro slavery in the Amazon region and the liberator of the Indian slaves.)

Chronologically, the first revolt against the Portuguese regime—instigated primarily by intellectuals—was the so-called revolt of the Beckmans, in Maranhão, in 1684. Tomás Beckman, a poet and lawyer dissatisfied with the policies of the Companhia de Comércio do Maranhão, a government monopoly, urged the people to revolt. He later traveled to Lisbon to explain his actions and obtain favors for the colony, only to be arrested there. But the revolt that best character-ized the intellectual panorama of Brazil was the "Inconfi-dência Mineira" in 1789, which not only united several na-tionally well-known men of letters, but also brought in French and North American influence. José Joaquim da Maia, a stu-dent, was chosen to make the first contacts with the United States while he was coming back from Europe, imbued with democratic ideas. His first action was to meet with Thomas Jefferson, of whom he asked cooperation for the independence movement that was to be started in Brazil against Portugal. Others joined him—Domingos Vidal Barbosa, José Alvares Maciel, Alvarenga Peixoto, Tomás Antônio Gonzaga, Cláudio Manuel da Costa, and students and poets. The only military person was Joaquim José da Silva Xavier (?–1792), the *Tiradentes* (Tooth-puller), who was presumably the only person in Brazil ever quartered after being executed by hang-ing.

This liberation movement was essentially a revolt against the excessive taxation of gold, called *derrama* [the king's share was one fifth]. But it was the first important movement to-ward Brazil's independence, which was achieved on Septem-ber 7th, 1822. Independence was the result of an accumula-tion of intellectual values, in which the Emperor did not have, historically or morally, any influence, although he was given credit for it by universal public opinion. And so it was that, nineteen years after independence, he was removed from power, and a governing junta was constituted by and led by men of letters. By then, Brazil considered herself a power capable of governing herself and of facing, as she did, grave international crises, such as threats of invasion and the war against Paraguay.

Negro slavery always incurred the intense opposition of the intellectual elite; among them were Antônio de Castro Alves, the poet of the slaves; José do Patrocínio, a Negro orator; Luis Gama, a poet and also a Negro; Ruy Barbosa and Joaquim Nabuco. An intellectual "front" was created, which had roots in colonial times, and it directed its interests to national problems. Fiery young men, who at times lived in almost total social anarchy, watched for signs of justice and progress in government and worked for a regenerated country. Attempts at reform, coming from all social levels and from every human condition, slowly created new social attitudes that made possible the solution of more and more distressing problems. One point appears very clear from this gradual social progress: Brazilians are volatile and contradictory by nature—understanding and suspicious, explosive and sentimental, and, by necessity, revolutionary. They reject at a given moment any situation that may tend to offend their patriotism.

The slaves in Brazil had a greater freedom than their African brothers, who were subjected to the tyranny of the *sobas* (chief of an African tribe) and the regime of the *aringas* (tribal fortification in Africa). For this reason, colored democracy in Brazil has a more ancient historical basis than is commonly thought, despite the royal decrees of the colonial period forbidding intermarriages of Indians or whites with Negroes. The children of slaves, who had been integrated with Brazilian social life, were the most active conspirators against the Empire, and the abolition of slavery in Brazil was achieved because of the demands of the Negro population.

In 1889, on the eve of the Republic, the intellectuals were fully responsible for sending into exile an old and extremely good Emperor, himself a poet and man of letters. All the great propagandists of the republican regime were men of high intellectual standing: Ruy Barbosa, José do Patrocínio Filho, Quintino Bocaiúva, and Silva Jardim. These and others like them, through their written and oral word, created the popular mood for the establishment of the republican form of government. They, not Brazilian people in general, understood that the Empire, defaced by the black stain of slavery, was weak, in a political crisis, and close to moral and economic chaos.

The role of artists as well as that of men of letters should also be emphasized in the spiritual progress of Brazil. In Minas Gerais, the popular sculptor Antônio Francisco Lisboa (1730–1814), better known as "o Aleijadinho" (*the Little Cripple*), carved in soapstone images of the prophets in the Baroque style, to adorn the churches. Our greatest painters are Pedro Americo, Vitor Meireles, and Cândido Portinari; the first two made use of battle themes, obtaining astonishing effects, while the last mentioned was in the modernistic movement. Aurelio de Figueiredo and Calisto painted their native landscapes. Our greatest musical expression in the nineteenth-century was that of Carlos Gomes, who made the name of Brazil known in Europe with the presentation of his operas *O Guaraní, O Escravo,* and others. *O Guaraní* represented an Indian hero, and *O Escravo,* as the name says, a Negro slave.

Today in Brazilian political life the influence of intellectuals has not diminished; on the contrary, with the universality of culture and the exploitation of subsidiary scientific resources, it tends to grow stronger. Nowadays it is spread by books, the newspapers, radio, and television, powerful media for reaching the popular mind, and thus is enlightening public opinion and educating far more widely than ever before in history.

Luiz Franco de Sá Bacellar

Literary and Cultural Trends in Brazil

D URING THE early conquest and territorial occupation of Latin America, the colonists and administrators sent out by the European countries were preoccupied with imitating literary or artistic fashions then current in the Old World. In the Spanish viceroyalties and the governments-general of the Portuguese colonies in Latin America, one finds that the European influence was imposed upon the Christianized natives not only in education and dress, but also in the construction of houses and churches. European influence was also dominant in literature and the arts.

In the Spanish and Portuguese colonies, Baroque literature had its highest expression in the writings of the Jesuits; for example, in Brazil, in the *Sermons* (*Sermões*) of Father Antônio Vieira (1608–1697); and in the reports that Father José de Anchieta (1534–1597) addressed to the Principal of the Jesuit Company in Rome.

"A Ilha da Maré" ("The Island of the Tide"), attributed by some critics to Teixeira Leite (1545–1618?), was a poem marked by great Gongoristic influence; and, like the works of Gregório de Matos (1633–1696), it proves the subservience of the colonial writers to European literary fashions.

With the beginning of the exploitation of gold resources in Minas Gerais, the so-called "Escola Mineira" appeared and gave to Brazil artists such as "O Aleijadinho," the Little Cripple (1730–1814), who is famous for his group of biblical prophets carved in soapstone on the grounds of the church in Congonhas do Campo in Minas Gerais as well as for his architectural work in several churches and chapels located in Ouro Prêto, Sabará, and other cities in Minas. The musicologist Kert Lange has also recently discovered a group of composers of recitations, oratories, cantatas, and other types of sacred music dating from the eighteenth century, whose scores were found in the sacristies of old churches of Minas Gerais.

Typical of examples of eighteenth-century literary works are lyric poems like *Marília do Dirceu*, by Tomás Antônio Gonzaga (1744–1807), and *Cartas Chilenas* (*Chilean Letters*), attributed to Cláudio Manuel da Costa (1729–1789). The *Cartas* are a satire in poetry on the Portuguese administration of Minas Gerais. Both poets took part in the "Inconfidência Mineira" (1789), one of the first political movements that attempted to liberate Brazil from Portuguese colonial rule.

The advent of the Encyclopedists and the French Revolution helped to create a French influence in Latin American literature. Representative types of that influence in Brazil are José Bonifácio (1765–1838); Father Bartolomeu Lourenço de Gusmão (1685–1724), who published sermons and historical and scientific works; and Antônio José da Silva (1705–1739), whose plays show the influence of Molière.

In 1808, Dom João fled from the French troops that were attacking Lisbon and took refuge in Brazil. His arrival there marked a new literary and artistic period in the Portuguese colony. The Le Breton Mission imported artists like Debret and Rugendas, who documented the Brazilian scenery and customs, and eventually influenced the educational efforts of Prince Regent Dom João, who founded the Royal Academy of Fine Arts in Rio de Janeiro.

With the advent of independence and the coronation of Dom Pedro, the son of Dom João, as emperor of Brazil in 1822, the influence of European Romanticism became more pronounced. A typically Latin American Romantic movement called "Indianism" appeared in Brazilian literature. Two of its most important proponents in Brazil were Gonçalves Dias (1823–1864) in poetry and José de Alencar (1829–1879) in prose.

In the nineteenth century, after the Spanish and Portuguese colonies in Latin America had achieved independence, the poets, writers, and intellectuals of those countries became concerned about creating nationalist literatures. Accordingly, poems like *La araucana* (although published in 1569, 1578, and 1589 in Madrid) and *Martín Fierro* (published in 1872, 1879 in Buenos Aires) were considered the highest expressions of literary nationalism of Chile and Argentina, respectively. Old narrations about pre-Columbian civilizations, such as those of the Inca Garcilaso (1539–1616) in Peru, were rediscovered. Mexican and Guatemalan scholars did research on old Aztecan and Mayan civilizations. Through their works, a number of Latin American writers did as José Martí (1853–1895) had done in Cuba and supported not only the political freedom and economic development of their countries but also the improvement of education and culture there.

Represented by writers like Eduardo Prado (1860–1901), author of *A Ilusão Americana,* and Monteiro Lobato (1882–1948), who translated and wrote several works about the international oil trust, a nationalistic literary movement in Brazil became evident. Immediately afterwards there appeared the novelists of the so-called "Ciclo do Nordeste," who described the underdevelopment and social and economic struggles in their regions. Among the writers of the "Ciclo do Nordeste" who should be mentioned are Jorge Amado (1912–   ), the novelist of the cacao plantations and the city of Bahia; and José Lins do Rêgo (1901–1957), who describes the struggle for survival of the small sugar mills (called *bangués*) against the huge mills installed by foreign enterprises; Graciliano Ramos (1892–1953); and Jorge de Lima (1893–1953), a poet whose work still has not been adequately appreciated by Brazilian critics.

The Parnassian and Symbolist literary movements, which originated in France, were imitated in Brazil, where they were to be attacked during the Modern Art Week celebrated in São Paulo in 1922. That year marks the liberation of Brazilian writers from the imitation of European literary patterns. This new development took place gradually, however, for movements such as the futurism of Marinetti (1876–1944), the Italian intellectual leader, continued to exert an influence on the decisions of the writers of São Paulo that led the movement. This is particularly true of Mário de Andrade (1893–1945) and Oswaldo Andrade (1890–1954), who intentionally broke with the old literary patterns, shocking the Paulista and other Brazilian middle classes in 1922 and the years that followed.

Among the principal poets of Brazilian modernism are Manuel Bandeira (1886–   ) of Pernambuco, and Carlos Drummond de Andrade (1902–   ) of Minas Gerais. The so-called "Generation of '45" brought forth a poet of the stature of João Cabral de Mello Neto of Pernambuco. His short play *Vida e Morte Severina*, with music by the young composer Chico Buarque de Holanda, was one of the greatest Brazilian theatrical successes in recent times.

ARTISTS AND WRITERS

IN

THE EVOLUTION OF LATIN AMERICA

Philosophy and Government

John H. Haddox

José Vasconcelos: Philosopher of Synthesis

THE APPROACH of philosophers in Latin America to problems of conduct has generally been profoundly humanistic. Of
all Latin-American philosophers perhaps none has been more
widely respected and influential and controversial than the
Mexican, José Vasconcelos (1882–1959), whose endeavors
ranged from politics and education to philosophy and letters.

As a student at the National Preparatory School Vasconcelos had supported Mexican President Porfirio Díaz and, for
a time, apparently accepted the teachings of positivist philosophy as presented by a group of ideologists for Díaz called
the *científicos*, the party of the scientists. This was natural
enough considering that through almost the entire youth of
Vasconcelos, President Díaz had been in power and all aspects of Mexican life, cultural and educational as well as economic and political, were controlled by the President and his
followers.

The fact that during the Díaz regime much of the Mexican
economy had come under foreign ownership and control, plus
the suppression of political opposition, led to widespread unrest. Finally, when in 1909 Díaz announced that he was running for office once again, Francisco Madero's battle cry
"sufragio efectivo; no reelección" won enough popular support to make the Revolution inevitable.

In the area of philosophy, positivism was the ideological
bulwark of the Díaz regime. The teachings of Auguste Comte,

French founder of the positivist philosophy, had been introduced into Mexico by the educator Gabino Barreda. In 1868 he opened the National Preparatory School as a center for Mexican positivism, which, in one form or another, was the dominant philosophical mode of thought until almost 1910.

Like Comte, Barreda saw positivistic philosophy, with its denial of metaphysics and theology and its exaltation of science, as the necessary instrument of social progress.

In 1892 the *científicos*, led by Justo Sierra and Francisco Bulnes, justified on "scientific grounds" the fourth reelection of Díaz, the so-called honest tyrant. Now the doctrines of Comte were modified by certain teachings of Charles Darwin and Herbert Spencer. The *científicos* argued that Darwin had shown that in the struggle for existence the fittest survive; Porfirio Díaz had survived three elections; hence, he was obviously the most fit to rule in his homeland.

By the time of Vasconcelos' graduation from law school, he was ready to join those opposed to the dictator. This was more than a mere change in political allegiance; he saw positivism not only as a defense of the dictatorship of Díaz, but also as an instrument for the expansion of economic interests from the United States, for the "anglicizing" of Mexico, and for the development of an empiricist-materialist philosophy.

On October 28, 1909, a group of approximately fifty young Mexican intellectuals, led by Antonio Caso, Pedro Henríquez Ureña (of the Dominican Republic), Alfonso Reyes, and José Vasconcelos came together to form the Ateneo de la Juventud. This organization had as its goals the destruction of Porfirism, the removal of foreign economic controls in Mexico, and the lessening of the influences of positivism on the cultural life and the educational system of Mexico. When the revolution against Díaz broke out in 1910, these Mexican *pensadores* attempted to formulate both an ideology of revolution and a plan for the cultural rehabilitation of the nation after the revolt.

At a meeting of the *Ateneo* in 1910 Vasconcelos presented a lecture entitled "Don Gabino Barreda y las ideas contemporáneas" in which he questioned Barreda's denial of artistic and metaphysical values and his excessive faith in the scientific method. He concluded: "The positivism of Comte and Spencer could never satisfy our aspirations."[1]

Vasconcelos then became a propagandist for the forces of Francisco I. Madero, who opposed Díaz. Eventually he had to flee to Washington, D. C., where he remained as a confidential agent for the Maderistas. After Díaz was overthrown, Vasconcelos returned to Mexico, beginning a long and active political career. Oswaldo Robles has noted that if Plotinus exercised a profound influence on the thought of Vasconcelos, it was Plato (with his ideal of a philosopher-king) who inspired his activities.[2]

In 1920, after brief periods as acting rector at the Universidad Nacional Autónoma de México and as Director of the Escuela Nacional Preparatoria, Vasconcelos began one of the most successful periods of his life. That year he was appointed Secretary of Public Education by President Alvaro Obregón. As Secretary he was in charge of schools, libraries, and fine arts. Because of his tireless efforts to reorganize and extend the educational system of Mexico and raise the general level of Mexican education, Vasconcelos has been credited with being the father of public education in Mexico. His political career did not end when he left this office in 1924. He ran unsuccessfully for the governorship of the state of his birth, Oaxaca, and then, in 1929, for the presidency of Mexico.

Vasconcelos had two reasons for involving himself in Mexican politics—one negative and one positive. On the one hand, he felt it his duty to resist the "triumph of the wicked, the imbeciles" in Mexican politics—to oppose corruption and tyranny in Mexico. On the other, he clearly felt from an early age that it was his duty to work for better living, working, and cultural conditions for the Mexican.

When Vasconcelos (who as a youth had participated in the titanic struggle against Porfirio Díaz, partly because of the latter's repeated reelections to the presidency) saw that Plutarco Elías Calles was in effect running for reelection (an action outlawed by the Constitution of 1917), using Pascual Ortiz Rubio as his puppet, he felt compelled to run for the office. What apparently started as a gesture of defiance rapidly escalated into a full-blown campaign.[3] It started in Nogales on November 10, 1928, when Vasconcelos demanded effective suffrage and no reelection. Despite an apparently extremely successful campaign, he went down to overwhelming defeat—at least according to the official returns, which gave Ortiz Rubio almost two million votes to Vasconcelos' approximately one hundred and eleven thousand. It was doubtless a fraudulent election; Calixto Maldonado declared: "Democracy has been assassinated; there were no elections. . . ." The Antireelecionista party president hopefully proclaimed that Vasconcelos had actually won a majority of the votes, hence was president-elect of Mexico.[4] Yet hopes for the eruption of another rebellion in Mexico, like that which deposed Díaz, were short-lived.

This defeat marked the end of Vasconcelos' active political career and the beginning of his life as a philosopher (though he had been interested in philosophy for many years and he never really lost his interest in the politics of Mexico, being always vitally interested in his country's proximate realities and more or less remote possibilities).

Vasconcelos created a complex philosophical system, including a theory of knowledge, a metaphysics, an ethics, and an esthetics called "esthetic monism."

Man is not a "pure spirit" or a "separated intellect," Vasconcelos insists. He is, in the Spanish phrase, *un hombre de carne y hueso* (a man of flesh and blood), so truth must be sought as the fruit of a total experience. One must seek the "whole" truth as a "whole" man.

It is said that Parmenides was being-intoxicated and Spinoza was God-intoxicated; it can equally well be said of Vasconcelos that he was unity-intoxicated. He was possessed by the desire to achieve comprehension of the totality of existence. He felt that most contemporary philosophers achieve at most a partial view of reality, because they fail even to consider the fullness of human experience. They ignore the emotions, utilizing only the senses and the intellect in their search for knowledge.

In contrast, the Mexican philosopher employed what he calls a "concurrent method," in which the senses, the intellect, and the emotions collaborate to achieve knowledge. In the collaboration of these organs each has its own function. The senses give knowledge its content, its material, its data. The intellect distinguishes and classifies this data by means of distinct concepts (like "green," "tall," "three," "square," etc.), but it is, of itself, cold and empty, lacking in vitality, purpose, and direction.

The tendency of the intellect is, Vasconcelos insisted, to break things down, to study parts, but what exists are whole things, not isolated parts. When a person attempts, by means of his intellect, to "explain" the qualitatively varied world that we experience through our senses, he does so by means of concepts. The knowledge so achieved is all on one abstract level, with much of the qualitative and substantial variety of our experience eliminated or ignored. Vasconcelos once commented that every philosophy based on generalities and abstractions, every philosophy of mere concepts, is like a crystal globe, beautiful but empty.[5]

He emphasized that the philosopher must respect the qualitative and substantial distinctions among things while, at the same time, organizing his experiences into a systematic picture of reality. This synthesis of the varied can be achieved, he felt, by means of an emotive knowledge (an emotion-informed intellect), because the emotions grasp the colors and the distinctions and the values of things and yet can unify these. The emotions, which tend to attract, to move, to unify diverse elements in so far as they are diverse, engender an enriched knowledge of the varied world we experience.[6] Esthetic knowledge, then, includes both facts and our feelings about these facts; and these feelings are all important in our lives—stirring us, attracting us, moving us to act. Yet they are too often neglected by philosophers, Vasconcelos felt.[7]

The knowledge this philosopher sought was a knowledge that "makes a difference" in our lives—a knowledge that enriches and gives value to what we think and what we do.

Vasconcelos rescues philosophy from the ubiquitous reputation of being impractical and irrelevant to the affairs of life. As was noted before, in addition to being a philosopher he was a man of action, an educator, and a political leader. In *¿Qué es la Revolución?* Vasconcelos insists that the philosopher must be a nonconformist, a social combatant, a politician. To use William James' term, he was, in this sense, a "tough-minded philosopher." He was never content to be a philosopher concerned with philosophical problems divorced from the world in which he lived; and this world was, for much of his life, the world of Mexican internal politics and external relations.

In his examination of social and political questions this philosopher was perhaps more concerned with what Mexico and the rest of Latin America *might* be than with what they are. (Although some knowledge of the actual present reality of this area is necessary for a projection of its potential future condition.) In any event, Vasconcelos wrote as a prophet.

Further, he approached these questions in a manner that was essentially constructive. In his *¿Qué es la Revolución?* Vasconcelos insisted that in every true revolution there is destruction only on the battlefield; every revolution must be short and thorough, and when it is over, the government must turn to peaceful, just, constructive action. He also remarked: "A revolution is the movement for a better way of life" and "a revolutionist is . . . anyone who adds a new treasure to the progress of mankind."[8]

Vasconcelos believed he had two treasures to give to mankind, especially the mankind of Mexico, in particular, and Latin America, in general. These treasures were the notion of a "cosmic race" and of "Bolivarism."

Concerning the first of these, his thesis, presented in a book entitled *La raza cósmica* (finished in 1925), was that the various races of the world tend to mix more and more as time goes on, to the benefit of mankind. In historical terms Vasconcelos noted that in Europe a mixture of races (including Greeks, Romans, Gauls, Celts, and Tuscans) produced "the fount of modern culture," and he expressed his conviction that the vigor and strength of the American is due to the fact that the United States has been a "melting pot" in which diverse nationalities and races have blended.[9] He ended this brief historical survey with these words: "In every case the highly optimistic conclusion which can be derived from these observations is that even the most contradictory mixtures can always be beneficially resolved because the spiritual factor in each serves to elevate the whole."

He was, thus, very much opposed to any theory that proposes the supremacy of a "pure race," and in several places he spoke most contemptuously of the Nazi party in Germany and the Ku Klux Klan in the United States.[10] (This book was published in the 1920's, but much of what he said is still relevant.) Contrary to the racist theories, according to which a mixture of bloods is considered to be degenerative, Vasconcelos seeks a vital renovation of mankind by means of racial synthesis. As a theoretical basis for this ideal he noted that according to the Mendelian laws of heredity the mating of contrary types will produce diverse and complex variations, and proclaimed that the variations will be superior to those that have existed previously if the mixture of races is in accordance with the laws of social harmony, sympathy, and beauty.[11] It will take time for the results of a mixture brought about, not by violence or force but through free choice founded on an aesthetic sense and love, to appear, but when (and if) they appear, their effect will be a period of true, universal brotherhood among men.

A basic assumption of the cosmic race theory is the essential equality of all men. This does not mean that all men are presently (or ever will be) equal in the sense of "identical" or "the same." Individual diversity of such things as nationality, race, color, intelligence, and artistic or commercial ability is compatible with an essential unity.

This assumption of the essential unity, along with the individual diversity of mankind, is traditional in Mexico. It extends back to the sixteenth century when Bishop Bartolomé de las Casas presented his arguments concerning the rights of the Indians. It has been incorporated into Mexico's various constitutions, and it determines policies of the present Mexican government. Never was this assumption so important as in the present day, when people in newly developing lands, often people of color, are realizing the injustice of political and social practices and institutions founded on assumptions of racial inferiority.

For Vasconcelos no race is inferior or superior to another in any general sense. Different races and nations develop strengths in different areas. Yet no race exists that is inherently lacking in the essential human characteristics or in special abilities which they can contribute to mankind. His emphasis on the compatibility of racial diversity and human unity contains a significant message for a world torn with racial strife.

Vasconcelos' "Bolivarism," was an expression of conviction

and hope for the future of Mexico and the rest of Latin America, despite the present turmoil.

In *Temas contemporáneos*, Vasconcelos explained that the Latin American nations are behind the United States in progress partly because the former were born prematurely of decadent parents (Spain and Portugal at the beginning of the nineteenth century), while the latter in a relatively mature state won her independence from a powerful motherland (England at that time).[12] He recognized that it would take Latin American nations more time to develop. He mentioned that as economic conditions improve, so will the political institutions and the cultural achievements of the Latin American nations. However, even Vasconcelos pleaded for political unity among Latin American nations, which he felt is actually required for economic development.

His point seems to be that the *United* States is powerful, while the *disunited* states of Latin America are weak. In unity there is strength, so in *¿Qué es la Revolución?* he expressed his hope that the Spanish-speaking nations of this hemisphere will be good neighbors among themselves as well as with the United States.

In a book entitled *Bolivarismo y Monroísmo* Vasconcelos praised and elaborated on the thesis presented in 1826 by Simón Bolívar at a conference of Latin American nations in Panama in which Bolívar called for the new Latin American republics to join in a political and economic union.

Vasconcelos began this book by distinguishing between Spanish Americanism and Pan-Americanism. "We call Bolivarism the Spanish American ideal of creating a federation of all the lands of Spanish culture; we call Monroism the Anglo-Saxon ideal of incorporating the twenty Hispanic nations in a North American empire achieved by the political means of Panamericanism."[13] Later, in *La raza cósmica*, he wrote of the

confrontation of Spanish America with the aggressive nationalism of European nations and the United States, again attacking both the Nazi party in Germany and the Ku Klux Klan
in the United States as secret racist organizations and, at the
same time, urging "the defense of our human patrimony."[14]
Thus Vasconcelos considered Bolivarism to be the strongest
force to oppose the domination of Latin America by either
European powers or "the colossus of the North."

However, fear of outside domination was not the most important reason for Vasconcelos' support of Bolivarism. He felt
that the lands of Latin America have a spiritual identity, as
well as national and political diversity. He believed that
heterogeneity had been emphasized too long and that the
time had arrived for a recognition of the relative cultural,
linguistic, and religious homogeneity of these nations. He
diagnosed, earlier than most, the ailments brought about by
hemispheric disunity, but he was fundamentally optimistic
about the future of a Latin America composed of nations that
desire more to cooperate intelligently than to compete ruthlessly.

Actually, it was not until after Vasconcelos wrote his
Bolivarismo y Monroísmo that an organization of nations that
are both independent, as separate nations, and interdepen-
dent, as *members* of such an organization—a system which
combines hemispheric unity with national diversity—was
formed. Such an organization, in aspiration and design, if not
yet in achievement, is the Organization of American States.
This organization, since it includes the United States, extends
beyond the boundaries of Vasconcelos' ideal expressed in
Bolivarismo y Monroísmo. However, Vasconcelos also enthu-
siastically supported relations between the United States and
Mexico based on the Good Neighbor concept, and therefore
both the approaches to Inter-American unity that were

strongly favored by the Mexican philosopher are combined in the O.A.S.

The problems—social, political, and, especially, economic—that face the nations of this hemisphere are enormous, but at least these nations are now (we hope) becoming more and more aware that their problems can be solved only by their united efforts.

As prophecy, the dreams of José Vasconcelos have at times failed to materialize. Yet who, in the face of the real and potential accomplishments of the Organization of American States, can deny that Vasconcelos was a true prophet of Latin America? José Gaos has suggested that perhaps one day the inhabitants of the lands of this hemisphere will speak of Vasconcelos as "the father of their spiritual homeland," as "precursor," and as "the genius of his race."

Vasconcelos was, then, at once a philosopher and a man of action with, in Agustín Basave's words, "an impatience for the eternal"; so he wrote books that were concerned primarily with philosophical questions (including his *Tratado de metafísica, Ética, Estética,* and *Lógica orgánica*) and others directed to social, political, and educational issues (including *La raza cósmica, Indología, Bolivarismo y Monroísmo, De Robinsón a Odiseo,* and *¿Qué es la Revolución?*). Yet, despite all this variety of activity, there was a remarkable unity of aim, a consistency of goal. This goal was to achieve a total *cosmovisión* wherein all the diversified aspects of reality would be unified while still diversified. As Oswaldo Robles says of Vasconcelos: "The philosopher does not have the myopic vision of an insect, but the telescopic vision of an eagle. The philosopher knows how to open his eyes to all the regions of existence. The philosophical spirit is not analytic; it is a spirit of synthesis."[15]

In José Vasconcelos the philosophical spirit pervaded every

aspect of thought. It was as essential to his view of the cosmic race—a synthesis of diverse bloods and cultures—and to his Bolivarism—a federation of Spanish American nations into one exemplary union—as it was to his metaphysic of esthetic monism—his theory of knowledge as attained by an emotion-informed intellect—and his ultimate goal of union with God while retaining personal identity.

Notes

[1] Antonio Caso, *et al.*, *Conferencias del Ateneo de la Juventud* (México, 1919), p. 7. For an excellent discussion of the activities of the *Ateneo de la Juventud*, see Patrick Romanell, "Bergson in Mexico: A Tribute to José Vasconcelos," *Philosophy and Phenomenological Research*, Vol. 21, No. 4 (June, 1961).

[2] Oswaldo Robles, "José Vasconcelos, el filósofo de la emoción creadora," *Filosofía y letras*, Vol. 13, No. 26 (April–June, 1947), p. 14.

[3] Vasconcelos' presidential campaign is described brilliantly by one of his aides, Mauricio Magdaleno, in *Las palabras perdidas* (México, 1956).

[4] John W. F. Dulles, *Yesterday in Mexico: A Chronicle of the Revolution* (Austin, 1961), p. 476.

[5] José Vasconcelos, *Indología* in *Obras completas*, 4 vols. (México, 1957–61), Vol. 2, p. 1119.

[6] Vasconcelos, *Lógica orgánica* in *Obras completas*, Vol 4, pp. 659–663.

[7] Vasconcelos, *Tratado de metafísica* in *Obras completas*, Vol. 3, p. 512.

[8] José Vasconcelos, *¿Qué es la Revolución?* (México, 1937), p. 93.

[9] Vasconcelos, *La raza cósmica* in *Obras completas*, Vol. 2, p. 905.

[10] Vasconcelos, *La raza cósmica*, p. 935.

[11] Vasconcelos, *La raza cósmica*, pp. 906–942.

[12] José Vasconcelos, *Temas contemporáneos* (México, 1956), p. 181.

[13] José Vasconcelos, *Bolivarismo y Monroísmo* in *Obras completas*, Vol. 2, p. 1305. Vasconcelos feels that there is a strong kinship among Latin American nations, stating in *El desastre* in *Obras completas*, Vol. 1, p. 1234, that they are "twenty sister nations bound together in language, race, and culture." In *Discursos*, made in 1920–1950 (México, 1950), p. 185, he exclaims: "Viva México, Viva Argentina, Viva Cuba [pre-Fidel], Viva Chile"; and in a grand voice, like a trumpet: "Viva Spanish America!"

[14] Vasconcelos, *La raza cósmica* in *Obras completas*, Vol. 2, pp. 1361–1379.

[15] Robles, "José Vasconcelos, el filósofo de la emoción creadora," p. 215.

Comments BY EDWARD H. MOSELEY

In his discussion of José Vasconcelos, Dr. Haddox has provided us with a link between the philosophical and artistic aspects of the Revolution. Historians are tempted to attack the views of Vasconcelos as groundless assertions or impractical dreams. His comments regarding *monroísmo* offer an inviting target for the political scientist trained in the German school. However, to challenge the historic interpretation of the great educator would be to miss his essential role in the history of Mexico. Vasconcelos provides one of the most outstanding examples of the influence of the *pensador* upon the political and social life of a Latin American nation. Not only did he ask "*¿Qué es la Revolución?*," but he worked actively to shape the future of that movement. He was an ardent advocate of the muralists, and gave extensive support to all fields of arts and letters. Perhaps his vision of *la raza cósmica* has proved visionary and impractical, but the ever-present *mexicanismo*, which is today a reality, owes its existence in great part to the pragmatic application of his ideals. Perhaps Vasconcelos can best be characterized as the propaganda agent and production manager of the changing Revolution.

The artists and philosophers have been charged with having distorted the Mexican Revolution. The same charge could be easily made against the politicians, the novelists, and even the ever "objective" historians. To assert that the Revolution has been distorted, however, implies that it is dead and a thing of the past. If this is not the case, and *la Revolución ya vive*, then the men of the arts and letters have played a very different role. They have assisted in its metamorphosis, advancing it into an institutionalized and idealized phase. Perhaps the mystical essence that is Mexico today, which grew out of the upheaval initiated in 1910, is better understood through an examination of the creative works of Diego Rivera and José Vasconcelos than the political works of Francisco Madero, Emiliano Zapata, or even the recently canonized Pancho Villa.

Daniel R. Reedy

The Cohesive Influence of José Carlos Mariátegui on Peruvian Art and Politics

Among the most prominent intellectual leaders of Spanish America during the twentieth century, José Carlos Mariátegui figures, by general concensus, at the forefront of the group. His position is due primarily to the positive force and lasting imprint of his personal actions and the avant-garde message of his essays, which captured the imagination of a large segment of Peru's population and won him considerable attention and esteem throughout Latin America, as well as in Europe. Professor Martin S. Stabb in his recent study on the Spanish American essay, entitled *In Quest of Identity* (1967), points up the importance of Mariátegui when he states that "José Carlos Mariátegui . . . has received the status of legend among Spanish American radicals."[1]

Although José Carlos Mariátegui's part as a founder of the Peruvian Socialist Party and as the author of the *7 ensayos de interpretación de la realidad peruana* (1928)[2] is well known, it should also be noted that he served an important function as a cohesive force in Peruvian politics and art during the decade from 1920 to 1930, when his country was beset by political turmoil and oppressed by a dictatorial government. This function was not a result of Mariátegui's avowed Marxism, it would seem, but rather for some almost indefinable personal force that seemed to emanate from him. One has only to talk with Mariátegui's associates of those years to discover that there was a certain mystique about him, which even those who knew him well cannot completely define. This personal magnetism of his, which has attracted all types of people (different not only in their political ideologies but also in their cultural and economic status) may be what Stabb has called Mariátegui's "mystical humanism."[3] Another term that might be used appropriately to define this aspect of Mariátegui's personality is the Greek word "charisma," which denotes an individual's personal magic of leadership and his capability of arousing special popular loyalty or enthusiasm. Unquestionably, Mariátegui did possess a kind of charismatic personality, for his role as a political and intellectual leader in Peru in the post World War I period is difficult to comprehend if an explanation is sought solely in the appeal of the Marxist doctrine which he so openly espoused.

The circumstances surrounding Mariátegui's birth, childhood, and early years give little indication of the influence he would later exercise. According to his most recent biographer, Mariátegui was born in Moquegua on June 14, 1894,[4] and although it is not stated in any source, there is the whispered suspicion that he, as well as his brothers and sisters, were born out of wedlock, though their parents most certainly did live together for a time as "convivientes." At the time of his birth, the only factor definitely in favor of any future success was his surname: he was a descendent of Francisco Javier Mariátegui, the secretary of Peru's First Constituent Congress. José Carlos' father, Francisco Mariátegui, was a minor government employee, while his mother, Amalia Lachira, was a mestiza from the province of Huacho.

José Carlos' father soon abandoned his wife and four children, leaving them with no funds to support themselves. Besides being a sickly child, at the age of seven José Carlos was struck a severe blow on his leg, and after a series of operations in a Lima hospital for the poor, he was left permanently crippled. There is every reason to believe, also, that the blow from the stone only aggravated a condition which already existed and was due to acute malnutrition.

By the age of fourteen Mariátegui was forced to end his formal studies and take a job to help support his family. He went to work in the typesetting office of *La Prensa,* a Lima newspaper, where by the age of seventeen he was advanced to the position of proofreader. In the offices of *La Prensa* Mariátegui made his first important friendships in Abraham Valdelomar, Félix del Valle, and César Falcón, with whom he would later collaborate in the journal *Colónida* (1916). It was also in *Colónida* that Mariátegui made his literary debut with three sonnets, which he published in different numbers of the journal.[5]

Mariátegui's gradual movement toward the political Left can be seen as early as 1916 when he and César Falcón left *La Prensa* to work for *El Tiempo,* a leftist daily. Mariátegui's career as a writer then began in earnest, since he was allowed to write on the national political situation for the editorial section of the paper. Also, with Félix del Valle, Mariátegui began his career as a publisher, organizing and publishing a politically-oriented journal called *Nuestra Epoca,* whose first and only number appeared in June of 1918.

Although these first editorial attempts did not meet with marked success, Mariátegui did not desist, and he soon enlisted the aid of César Fálcon and Humberto del Aguila to found *La Razón,* a leftist-oriented daily, in 1919. In *La Razón,* Mariátegui began to search for a clearer definition of his socialist ideas as he expounded on and defended them in the columns of his newspaper. It is apparent that his socialist activity really began with *La Razón,* in which he defended the workers' movement of 1919 and the Peruvian university reform. Also, with César Falcón he was instrumental in founding the Comité de Propaganda Socialista for which *La Razón* served as the propaganda outlet. Mariátegui's growing sphere of political activities, particularly his influence among the working classes, did not go unnoticed by the newly installed government of Augusto B. Leguía, and the publication of *La Razón* was abruptly suspended in July of 1919 shortly after Leguía came to power, thus terminating what Mariátegui had called "el periódico del pueblo y para el pueblo."[6]

The following four and one-half years in Mariátegui's life, from 1919 to 1923, were to have a profound influence on his intellectual development and on the subsequent course of events in Peruvian history during the major part of the decade of the twenties. After Leguía's take-over in 1919, there was an immediate attempt to find means of ridding the country of political activists and potential troublemakers. Consequently, César Falcón, Félix del Valle, and José Carlos Mariátegui were offered government scholarships for study in Europe. Leguía's means of getting a potential enemy of the government out of Peru permitted Mariátegui to travel to Europe, where he was to learn about the Socialist movement in greater depth. On his arrival in Paris, Mariátegui wasted no time in contacting socialist leaders, among them Henri Barbusse; and shortly thereafter in Italy, where he was to remain for two and one-half years, he attended meetings of the Italian Socialist Party and witnessed at first-hand the birth of Fascism and the rise of Mussolini. He also studied, wrote, and made personal contacts with some of the most influential intellectuals of the time: Croce, D'Annunzio, Marinetti, Gorki, and numerous others. Toward the end of his stay in Europe he traveled to Germany and hoped to continue on to Russia, but family responsibilities (he had married in Italy and had a young son) and a lack of money prevented his realization of that desire.

On his return to Peru in March of 1923, Mariátegui was cooly received by many of his former friends, who felt that his having accepted a scholarship from Leguía's government was traitorous. However, it was Víctor Raúl Haya de la Torre (often called simply Haya), the founder of the Aprista Party and its present leader, who was instrumental in drawing Mariátegui back into the mainstream of Peruvian political activity. At first Haya urged Mariátegui to aid in the battle against Leguía's government and the Church in their concerted effort to consecrate Peru to the Sagrado Corazón de Jesús. Although Mariátegui refused to participate in the battle, Haya did manage to gain his participation in the Universidades Populares González Prada, and he also introduced him to many of the young activists in the Federación Estudiantil del Perú, which Haya had organized earlier.

An alliance between Mariátegui and Haya de la Torre gradually developed, in part from their personal sympathy and admiration for each other, and in part because of their common political and revolutionary cause. This alliance had the effect of creating, for the first time, a solid front for the Leftist movement in Peru, and although it lasted but a few short years, it served to bind together various factional elements in their active opposition to Leguía's dictatorial regime. Following Haya de la Torre's expulsion from the country in October of 1923, Mariátegui became the principal leftist figure remaining in Peru. Haya had recognized Mariátegui's potential as a leader of the Left, and before leaving Peru, he turned over to him the editorship of his newly formed journal, *Claridad,* which rapidly became a symbol of the nascent unity between political factions, laborers, and students. In this new activity, Mariátegui was soon actively collaborating with future Aprista leaders still resident in Peru, among them Luis Alberto Sánchez, Manuel Seoane, Carlos Manuel Cox, and Luis Heysen.

It should be noted at the same time that Mariátegui did not completely isolate himself from the more conservative elements in Lima's intellectual circles. Clemente Palma, the

editor of the important journal *Variedades*, enlisted Mariátegui as a feature writer for the journal, and during a brief
period of time José Carlos wrote for *Variedades* a number of
significant essays, which would later appear in his books *La
escena contemporánea* (1925) and *El alma matinal . . .*
(1950).[7]

It was not, however, Mariátegui's adroit political leadership
that so firmly ensconced him at the head of the leftists, but a
personal crisis in his life. In 1924 he again entered the hospital,
and his right leg, which had seemed to be sound, was ampu-
tated. The effect of this illness and the amputation of his leg
produced in Mariátegui a nervous crisis marked by increased
anxiety and fear that he might die before he could fulfill his
mission. From that point in his life, he began to work with a
greater sense of urgency than ever before. His precarious economic situation and the hospital fees prompted a benevolent
movement among his friends and acquaintances to aid him
financially during that moment of crisis. María Wiesse, a close
friend of Mariátegui, has recalled that moment in his life, and
she describes the actions of his friends:

> . . . un hermoso movimiento de solidaridad fraterna se produce
> entre intelectuales y artistas del Perú. Escritores de las más
> diversas ideologías, artistas de distintas tendencias, estudiantes,
> obreros, aportaron su ayuda al compañero en las horas difíciles
> que atravesaba.[8]

This humanitarian act, initiated by the future Aprista stal-
wart Luis Alberto Sánchez, served to win for Mariátegui the
personal sympathy of a major portion of Lima's intellectuals
of both the Right and the Left, as well as the compassion of
the general public, which considered Mariátegui as the champion of its welfare. Since Mariátegui was practically confined
to his home at 544 Washington Street, his study became a
place of daily reunion for intellectuals and artists of what he
called the "Peruvian vanguard."

Although he had not been able to realize his plan immediately after returning from Europe, Mariátegui had continued to dream of organizing a journal that would bring together the writers and artists of the "Vanguardia." In an interview in *Variedades* in June of 1925, Mariátegui described this project as a journal of literary criticism for the writers and artists of the Peruvian and Spanish American vanguard.[9] His vanguard journal was born in September 1926, not with the title originally considered, but with one which captured a certain nationalistic spirit, an indigenous connotation, a hint of the teacher and leader of people: *Amauta*, a title which was suggested to him by the Peruvian indigenous painter José Sabogal.[10]

In the first issue of *Amauta*, Mariátegui elaborated on his conception of the new journal and told something of its scope and purpose, which was to emphasize the contemporary movements in politics, philosophy, literature, art, and science. Mariátegui wrote:

> Esta revista, en el campo intelectual, no representa un grupo. Representa, más bien, un movimiento, un espíritu. En el Perú se siente desde hace algún tiempo una corriente, cada día más vigorosa y definida, de renovación. A los fautores de esta renovación se les llama vanguardistas, socialistas, revolucionarios, etc. La historia no los ha bautizado definitivamente todavía. Existen entre ellos algunas discrepancias formales, algunas diferencias psicológicas. Pero por encima de lo que los diferencia, todos estos espíritus ponen lo que los aproxima y mancomuna: su voluntad de crear un Perú nuevo dentro del mundo nuevo. . . . El movimiento—intelectual y espiritual—adquiere poco a poco organicidad. Con la aparición de "Amauta" entra en una fase de definición.
>
> ❀ ❀ ❀
>
> El objeto de esta revista es el de plantear, esclarecer y conocer los problemas peruanos desde puntos de vista doctrinarios y científicos. . . . Estudiaremos todos los grandes movimientos de

renovación—políticos, filosóficos, artísticos, literarios, científicos.
Todo lo humano es nuestro. Esta revista vinculará a los hombres
nuevos del Perú, primero con los de los otros pueblos de
América, en seguida con los de los otros pueblos del mundo.[11]

It took Mariátegui very little time to set about realizing the
purpose which he outlined in *Amauta's* first number. He began
corresponding with young writers from all of Peru's provincial
centers. He enlisted the efforts of the *indigenistas* from Cuzco,
Arequipa, and Puno, and the young revolutionary poets from
Huancayo and Huánuco in the central sierra; in the northern
towns of Trujillo and Chiclayo he solicited the collaboration
of the contemporaries and followers of César Vallejo, and in
Lima he brought together the young literary intelligentsia of
diverse tendencies, including writers of previous generations,
such as the poet José María Eguren, whose works were revi-
talized through the pages of *Amauta*.[12] Mariátegui's house was
more than ever the intellectual, political, and literary center of
Lima. There were daily gatherings of writers, artists, politicians, and common laborers, who came to discuss innumerable topics. Many of these same topics were expounded upon
by Mariátegui in his essays in *Amauta,* and some were later
incorporated into his *7 ensayos de interpretación de la realidad peruana* (1928).

From the broad scope of Mariátegui's essays in *Amauta,* as
well as those which he published in *Variedades* and *Mundial,*
it is easy to see why he was able to attract people to him. He
wrote on politics, literary criticism and theory, art, international problems, Peruvian economics, the problem of the
Indian, and numerous other subjects. These essays were collected into two volumes, published during his lifetime—*La
escena contemporánea*[13] (1925) and the *7 ensayos* (1928).
Mariátegui's collected writings, written and published in various journals between 1914 and his death in 1930, now number
eight volumes.[14]

Amauta's publication was interrupted only once, when several of the journal's collaborators were arrested, and subsequently exiled, as a result of what the government termed a Communist plot.[15] Mariátegui himself was placed under police custody, in a hospital because of his poor health. A police raid on the printing shop where *Amauta* was published had netted several inflammatory letters written by exiles, and the journal's publication was suspended by Leguía's government from June until December of 1927, when growing adverse reaction from intellectuals throughout the Western Hemisphere and Europe prompted the government to reconsider its earlier action. Even though the most militant of his collaborators were sent into exile, Mariátegui returned to his task with greater urgency, immediately enlisting the aid of writers still in Peru, while those in exile throughout Europe and Spanish America mailed him their contributions. In a sense, the government's oppressive action only served to make *Amauta* grow in influence and prestige.

The strong personal and ideological affinity which had existed between Mariátegui and Haya de la Torre—the cohesive force which had held the Peruvian Leftists together— was broken finally in 1928 when Mariátegui wrote Haya in care of the Aprista cell in Mexico to protest the formation of the APRA as a "party" rather than an "alliance," which Mariátegui felt would have better represented the interests of all the political Left instead of just a segment of it.[16] Haya de la Torre's prompt reply in a letter dated the 20th of May forced a complete break between the two men. The Aprista leader accused Mariátegui of being infested with "tropical demagoguery" and warned him:

> No pierda la fé. No se caiga en la izquierda o en el izquierdismo (zurdismo lo llamo yo) de los literatos de la revolución. Póngase en la realidad y trate de disciplinarse no con Europa revolucionaria sino con América revolucionaria. . . . Ya sé que

está Ud. contra nosotros. No me sorprende. Pero la revolución
la haremos nosotros sin mencionar el socialismo pero repartien-
do las tierras y luchando contra el imperialismo.[17]

No reply was ever forthcoming from Mariátegui to Haya de
la Torre.

Within a few months of the break with Haya and the
Apristas, Mariátegui was instrumental in founding the Partido
Socialista Peruano (September, 1928), which he directed until his death. In addition to his purely political activities, Mariátegui also organized a bimonthly newspaper, *Labor*, which
first appeared in November of 1928. Since it was particularly
directed at the Peruvian laborers and *campesinos*, the Leguía
regime feared repercussions from it, and it was closed after
the September, 1929, number. A renewed attack was com-
menced against *Amauta* also, and Mariátegui finally decided
that he could no longer continue his work in Peru. Just before
his death he made plans to move to Buenos Aires, where
greater freedom of expression was promised, but Mariátegui's
time had run out. His old illness recurred in March of 1930,
and death came to him in Lima on the 16th of April. *Amauta*
also died, almost simultaneously with Mariátegui. Three
numbers of the journal appeared after his death, under the
direction of Ricardo Martínez de la Torre, but with Mariátegui gone, the cohesive substance which kept many of
Amauta's writers united also disappeared. Perhaps, however,
as one writer has suggested, *Amauta* did not die because
Mariátegui was gone, but because it had already accomplished its mission.[18]

The influence of Mariátegui and his journal has not yet
dissipated, even four decades after their physical disappear-
ance. *Amauta* still stands as a kind of fraternal bond among
the writers who collaborated in it, even though they have
since been divided at times by the force of political orienta-

tion. Writers such as Xavier Abril, a poet of some consequence, a close associate of Mariátegui, and a collaborator in
Amauta, has captured something of Mariátegui's contribution
to that generation. He says:

> Casi toda mi generación se salvó con el ejemplo de su vida
> que era su propia dialéctica. Mi generación, que pudo perderse
> en el más desenfrenado subjetivismo estético, debido a la bús-
> queda desesperada de la razón en la psiquis . . . se salvó a la
> temperatura afirmativa y revolucionaria de su materialismo.
> Y en ello había mucho de ese espíritu nacido de la lucha social,
> de la angustia creadora. . . .
>
> No exageré una vez cuando dije que el *Perú Nuevo*
> le debía [a Mariátegui] su nacimiento.[19]

And the charismatic force of Mariátegui's personality is also
echoed in the words of Angela Ramos, who first met Mariátegui in the offices of *La Prensa* in 1918. She sums up, in a
way, Mariátegui's personal effect on the individuals who knew
him, when she says:

> José Carlos me enseñó a pensar, a saber que venía un mundo
> distinto del que vivíamos en aquellos días.
>
> Mariátegui ha sido el hombre más extraordinario que conocí
> en mi vida, y creo que no volveré a conocer otro igual.[20]

These comments are largely representative of those concerning the truly remarkable influence of José Carlos Mariátegui
on Peruvian politics and all aspects of that country's intellectual life during the decade of the twenties. In effect, Mariátegui achieved what no other figure has been able to do in
Peru, either before him or since. Through the pages of his
journal and his personal leadership, he fought against the
nineteenth-century conservatism and traditionalism of his
country and attempted to expose the people to the stark
realities of twentieth-century life and thought. Mariátegui
and *Amauta* served as an undeniable cohesive force in the

vanguard movement of art and politics, which would lead the way to greater enlightenment among Peruvians in all areas of human interest.

Notes

[1] Martin S. Stabb, *In Quest of Identity. Patterns in the Spanish American Essay of Ideas, 1890–1960* (Chapel Hill, 1967), p. 111.

[2] See Note 14.

[3] Stabb, *In Quest of Identity. Patterns in the Spanish American Essay of Ideas, 1890–1960*, p. 118.

[4] Guillermo Rouillón, *Bio-bibliografía de José Carlos Mariátegui* (Lima, 1963), p. 9. Rouillón points out that earlier biographers erred in stating that Mariátegui was born in Lima in 1895.

[5] Eugenio Chang-Rodríguez, *La literatura política. De González Prada, Mariátegui y Haya de la Torre* (México, 1957), p. 131.

[6] María Wiesse, *José Carlos Mariátegui. Etapas de su vida* (Lima, 1945), p. 34.

[7] See Note 14.

[8] Wiesse, *José Carlos Mariátegui. Etapas de su vida*, p. 66.

[9] "¿Qué prepara usted?" in *Variedades*, 9th year, No. 901, June 6, 1925. Pages are unnumbered and no author is given for this article.

[10] Genaro Carnero Checa, *La acción escrita. José Carlos Mariátegui periodista* (Lima, 1964), p. 187.

[11] José Carlos Mariátegui, "Presentación de 'Amauta'," *Amauta*, 1st year, No. 1 (September, 1926), p. 3.

[12] No. 21 of *Amauta* (February–March, 1929) was dedicated by Mariátegui to articles on José María Eguren and his poetic works. Mariátegui, himself, prepared one of the essays which later appeared in his *7 ensayos*.

[13] See Note 14.

[14] Carnero Checa, *La acción escrita. José Carlos Mariátegui periodista*, p. 20. This source states that Mariátegui's first article appeared in *La Prensa* on Jan. 1, 1914. Volumes of Mariátegui's essays published during his lifetime were *La escena contemporánea* (1925) and the *7 ensayos de interpretación de la realidad peruana* (1928). Published after his death was *El alma matinal y otras estaciones del hombre de hoy* (1950), plus five other volumes published by the Empresa Editora Amauta in Lima as part of the *Obras completas*, 8 vols. (Lima, 1925–1959). The three aforementioned volumes constitute Vols. 1–3 of this edition, plus the following: Vol. 4, *La novela y la vida* (1955); Vol. 5, *Defensa del marxismo* (1959); Vol. 6, *El artista y la época* (1959); Vol. 7, *Signos y obras* (1959); and Vol. 8, *Historia de la crisis mundial* (1959).

[15] *El Comercio*, June 8, 1927, p. 4. Follow-up reports on the arrests appeared in *El Comercio* on June 9, 10, and 12.

[16] Wiesse, *José Carlos Mariátegui: Etapas de su vida*, p. 112.

[17] Ricardo Martínez de la Torre, *Apuntes para una interpretación marxista de la historia social del Perú*, Vol. 2 (Lima, 1948), pp. 298–299.

[18] Alberto Tauro, "Biografía de 'Amauta'," in *Amauta y su influencia* (Lima, 1960), p. 12.

[19] Xavier Abril, "Idea de la salvación revolucionaria del hombre," in *Poemas a Mariátegui* (Lima, 1959), p. 160.

[20] Eduardo Calvo, "Palomilla de la literatura," *Caretas*, 16th year, No. 344, Dec. 21–Jan. 10, 1967, p. 48.

Comments BY RAY F. BROUSSARD

One of the important intellectual developments of the early twentieth century in Latin America was the vanguardian or futurist movement. Sometimes called Arielists to indicate their debt to José Enrique Rodó, the members of this new movement found expression in most countries in a surge of national pride and sense of mission. Sparked by the university reform movement, the leaders of the Arielists, also known as the Generation of 1910, vowed to remake and regenerate their countries. By this, they usually meant to bring about social and economic reforms which would dismantle the aristocratically controlled status quo and elevate the masses to a higher place in life.

In countries with large Indian populations the problems faced were particularly acute. Vanguardists sought ways and means to incorporate these exploited people into the mainstream of national life. Thus we have in countries such as Bolivia, Ecuador, and Peru the development of Indiophiles or Indianists among the futurists or vanguardists.[1]

Professor Reedy has aptly chosen one of the leading Indianists of Peru for the subject of his paper. He would have had to search long and far to find one better adapted to the theme of this conference. Most Indianists of Peru, like the precursor of José Carlos Mariátegui, González Prada, or contemporaries like Antenor Orrego and Luis E. Valcárcel, were idealists and scholars. They were influenced by Spengler's thesis that Western Europe and the United States were in a state of inevitable decline. As Western culture decayed, they expected a new and vital mestizo civilization to arise from its ashes. The values and inspirations for this new world were to come from the spirit of the ancient Inca.[2]

As is pointed out so ably in this well-constructed and thoroughly researched study, Mariátegui worked with this group of Peruvian idealists. He was their inspiration, their leader, and he provided them with a vehicle, his journal *Amauta*, for the expression of their ideas. Had he accomplished nothing more than this, he would merit the praise lavished upon him by historians, but Mariátegui went much further to give substance and direction to the academic theories of his fellow Indianists. His ideas, which are well known, as Dr. Reedy points out, were more concrete and practical than those of his fellow vanguardists. He was the first of the Indianists to cast his thoughts into a definite political mold, which, according to Robert McNicoll, is why he was important in preparing the road for Aprismo.[3]

Mariátegui saw the problem of his country as primarily that of land tenure, but in projecting a solution he opposed normal agrarian reform techniques because he was convinced they were unworkable in Peru. He saw the economy of his country as feudalistic, not capitalistic. He frankly admitted that he was interested in the Indians because of the *ayllus*, a group of related families that had held land in a communal pattern under the Inca empire. These *ayllus* had been destroyed by the colonial regime, and Mariátegui hoped to resurrect them. In other words he looked to the old Incan spirit of cooperation—Incan socialism, he called it—as the system which was best adapted to the country as a whole. For Mariátegui, therefore, *indigenismo* and socialism were inseparable.[4]

Mariátegui's preoccupation with socialism was profoundly influenced by his Marxism, a point mentioned but not emphasized in Dr. Reedy's study. Mariátegui's knowledge of the dialectic and the materialistic interpretation of history gave a clearer and more pragmatic cast to his essays on the Indian problem. He is described by Rex Crawford as a "scientific radical" and by Frederick Pike as the most original Peruvian intellectual of the twentieth century. Marxism led Mariátegui to scorn the narrow nationalism of many of his contemporaries. He viewed his mission not only as the regeneration of Peru, but also as part of a world movement to rescue oppressed peoples everywhere. Can this be the reason for the estrangement between Mariátegui and Víctor Raúl Haya de La Torre, the founder of Aprismo? As related in the paper by Doctor Reedy, Mariátegui objected to Haya de La Torre's organization of APRA as a political party dedicated to revolution in Peru only. He objected to the definition of its objectives in a national and regional sphere. In his reply to this criticism, Haya de la Torre agreed that his movement was nationalistic and regional, and he warned Mariátegui against involvement in the European revolution at the expense of American revolutionary movements. In his closing remarks the founder of Aprismo called for agrarian reform, which Mariátegui had endorsed. On the other hand, he rejected socialism, a position which Mariátegui could hardly accept.

Dr. Reedy says that the break was final and that Mariátegui did not reply to Haya de la Torre. While it is true that no reconciliation took place, there is an indication that the rupture might not have been permanent had Mariátegui lived, for the two men were ideologically very close. In a footnote to his work *7 Ensayos*, published the same year he broke with APRA, Mariátegui wrote,

> After having finished this book, I found in Haya de la Torre's book, *Toward the Emancipation of Latin America*, ideas that are in agreement with my own on the agrarian question in general and on the Indian community in particular. We start from the same point of view, so that necessarily our conclusions must be the same.[5]

Mariátegui's connection with Aprismo cannot be lightly dismissed. Professor Reedy says that he had an "unwritten alliance" with Haya de la Torre and describes their work together in the student protest movement and particularly in the González Prada Popular University. During this period there was no doubt that Haya de la Torre was the leader, the political activist, while Mariátegui was still the essayist and thinker. Then came exile for the future organizer of Aprismo. When Haya de la Torre left Peru, he looked about for someone to carry on his work. He chose his colleague for the editorship of his journal *Claridad* and thus propelled Mariátegui into a position of leadership among the radical Left. The decade of the 1920's was a period of harsh political dictatorship in Peru. All political parties were abolished and most opposition leaders were exiled or imprisoned. It was during this dark hour that Mariátegui organized *Amauta*, the literary journal which served as the cohesive force in Peruvian revolutionary radicalism, as Dr. Reedy has pointed out in his paper. Mariátegui unified the radicals, particularly those with Indianist ideas. Many of these men later joined APRA and still speak of the editor of *Amauta* with husky, reverent voices and tear-filled eyes. Few people today dispute the intellectual debt which Aprismo owes to Mariátegui.[6]

With such an important connection between Mariátegui and Aprismo, it seems necessary to refer once more to Mariátegui's estrangement from the movement. Could it have been merely the result of temperamental differences only, as suggested by Crawford,[7] or is it possible that there were other reasons for the separation? Another possible answer to the puzzle is to attribute the break to Mariátegui's Marxist orientation. It should be noted that at almost the same time that he was moving away from Haya de la Torre, he seemed to be involving himself more in political activism. No longer was he the relatively harmless radical intellectual who was publishing a scholarly literary journal. Mariátegui founded the bimonthly newspaper *Labor* which wooed laborers and *campesinos*. This was direct political activity. The new periodical so alarmed the Leguía government that Mariátegui was arrested and both his newspaper and literary journal were suppressed. It was also at this time that Mariátegui organized the Marxist-oriented Peruvian Socialist Party.

But what of this Marxism of Mariátegui? Certainly it was a curious brand, with its emphasis upon Incan socialism. A deviation from communist orthodoxy, it definitely did not follow the Moscow party line. Mariátegui rejected communist materialism and predicted that Marxian socialism would not provide the inspiration for the move toward Peruvian socialism. Instead, he predicted that the spirit would come from the pride in the glories of past Incan accomplishments.[8]

In conclusion, it might be interesting to speculate upon the course of Mariátegui's further development had he lived longer. There seemed to be a hardening of his communist idealism by 1928, as evidenced by his break with Aprismo and his founding of the Peruvian Socialist Party. The year of his death, and (note) only after his death, this party affiliated with the Communist International.[9] Would it have done so had its founder still been alive to control and direct it in the channels of his peculiar brand of Marxian Indianism or Peruvian socialism? Or, would he have broken with the Communist and thrown in his lot with Aprismo, as he saw some of his revolutionary theories actually being carried out during the next decade? We can give no answers to such questions except to note that many of Mariátegui's ideas have been preserved and incorporated into the platform of APRA. Thus, we must join Professor Reedy in his evaluation of José Carlos Mariátegui as a cohesive force in the vanguard movement of art and politics of Peru and agree with him that the influence of this great essayist and political philosopher has not yet dissipated even four decades after his death.

Notes

[1] Frederick B. Pike, *The Modern History of Peru* (London, 1967), pp. 205 and 233.

[2] Robert McNicoll, "Intellectual Origins of Aprismo," *Hispanic American Historical Review*, Vol. 23 (1943), p. 430.

[3] McNicoll, "Intellectual Origins of Aprismo," p. 423.

[4] José Carlos Mariátegui, "El problema de la tierra" in *Antología de José Carlos Mariátegui*, ed. Benjamín Carrión (México, 1966), p. 5–8.

[5] José Carlos Mariátegui, *7 Ensayos de interpretación de la realidad peruana* (1928) as quoted by William Rex Crawford in *A Century of Latin American Thought* (Cambridge, Mass., 1961), p. 188.

[6] McNicoll, "Intellectual Origins of Aprismo," p. 432.

[7] Crawford, *A Century of Latin American Thought*, p. 188.

[8] Pike, *The Modern History of Peru*, p. 237.

[9] Pike, *The Modern History of Peru*, p. 237.

Federico G. Gil

Ideology and Pragmatism: The Crisis in Chilean Christian Democracy

A PEOPLE well known for their independence and temperance of character, who have little sentimentality and a great dose of pragmatism in their general approach to life, the Chileans have never produced outstanding "ideologists" or political *pensadores* or any political leader with a systematic and integrated political "theory." Eduardo Frei, whose claim to intellectual leadership in his own country cannot be contested, has himself stated that as social thinkers, Chileans "have been great imitators of history and ideas of other peoples."[1] It must be said that in this respect, Chile is not an exceptional case, although it is one in which this historical circumstance emerges perhaps most distinctly within the Latin American scene; for in general the region is characterized by a pattern in which ideological conflicts among its elites have always reflected the ideologies of Europe. Thus, in the past, liberal thought in Latin America tended to mirror images of the positivism and anticlericalism of the European radicals, just as conservative elites in the area reflected faithfully the conservatism of the European landowning feudal class. Latin American leaders who have engaged in a search for native cultural roots are few in number.

Noted exceptions are the attempts of Mariátegui, Luis Alberto Sánchez, and Haya de la Torre to reassess the importance of aboriginal civilizations, building at the same time

155

a theory of Indo-America as a distinct cultural entity. In addition there has been the relatively successful effort of the Mexican Revolution, exemplified by José Vasconcelos' *raza cósmica* (cosmic race), to glorify the accomplishments of the pre-Columbian civilizations and to integrate the Indian into the national culture. Even in Latin America, modern nationalism, with precious few exceptions, has not led to a significant revival of interest in autochthonous culture, although a few contemporary leaders in the continent may have called upon Latin America to make its distinctive contribution to world civilization.[2] Instead, modern nationalism has put the emphasis on the drive for social reform and opposition to imperialism, aiming at such goals as economic development through planning, industrialization, the expansion of educational opportunity, strong and efficient government, and an end to party strife.

These observations, however, should not be construed as meaning that Chile has not been represented with some distinction among the ranks of Latin American *pensadores* or social philosophers who, with grave concern for their continent, analyzed the biological elements of their society and made most forthright and bitter attacks upon their country's political and economic institutions. It is far from our intent to fail to recognize in their true measure the notable contributions of such men as Andrés Bello (1781–1865), native Venezuelan but Chilean by adoption, often referred to as "the greatest Spanish humanist since the Renaissance"; José Victorino Lastarria (1817–1888), doctrinaire exponent of rationalism and positivism and creator of Chilean progress and independence in thought; the fiery Francisco Bilbao (1823–1865) whose *Sociabilidad Chilena* (*The Nature of Chilean Society*) has been compared to the *Communist Manifesto* of 1848; or Valentín Letelier (1852–1919), the gentle educator influenced by Comte, Lacombe, and Durkheim. These men were powerful agents in the intellectual movement which began in 1842, destined to have significant consequences in Chile's political life. A new political group, the Liberal Party, arose in 1849 as an outgrowth of this intellectual renaissance. In 1850, another political group, the *Sociedad de la Igualdad* (Society of Equality) was established by Bilbao. Equalitarians and liberals joined forces against the ruling elite. During this period Santiago Arcos, a young disciple of French utopian socialism and an early champion of social reform, was the first national writer to study Chilean society in a systematic manner.

The significant point is that these Chilean thinkers, as well as those who followed their footsteps, were thoroughly European in their culture and gave scant attention to indigenous aspects of the Latin American environment. This thorough Europeanization of Chile's *pensadores*, past and present, reflected the slow but consistent amalgamation of diverse European groups with Amerindians, which has produced Chile's highly homogeneous culture. It also reflects the political patterns that the country has developed, which are so different from those of its neighbors. Among the Latin American republics Chile is the only one with its political forces clearly and distinctly aligned, as in many European countries, into three great blocs: the Right, the Center, and the Left. The resemblance of the Chilean political spectrum to that of much of Europe has been noted by many observers. "Chilean politics are undoubtedly more nearly 'European' than is the case elsewhere in Latin America."[3] All major parties, in their ideology as well as in their organization, behavior, and "style," exhibit European traits.

On the right of the party spectrum the Conservatives and the Liberals, now grouped under the Partido Nacional (PN), have accepted liberal democratic institutions and proclaimed adherence to the system of free enterprise, with religious issues still playing an important role in political thought. Its core has been the high-status groups—the socially notable—and the taproot of their strength is chiefly rural, with some representation of the lower-middle and urban working classes.

The Center is occupied by the Radical Party, traditionally the medium of political expression of Chile's middle class. During its early period, the Radicals subscribed to an orthodox nineteenth-century liberal point of view, deeply influenced by the ideals of French and Italian radicalism. Like its precursors in France and Italy, Chilean radicalism emerged as a reaction against oligarchical authoritarianism and as a defense of individual liberty. In the first part of the twentieth century it developed a collectivist orientation to meet the demands for social justice made by the lower segments of the Chilean population. Suffering from a basic schizophrenia since its inception, the Radical Party has always included a leftist branch, which advocated a socially oriented position close to socialism, and a rightist wing that identified its political philosophy with that of Conservatives and Liberals.[4] This division has resulted in vague, undefined ideology and expedient programs.

The Chilean Left consists of a coalition, *Frente de Acción Popular* (FRAP), chiefly composed of the Communist and Socialist Parties. The Communists, essentially a workers' party, are probably the most effective group of its kind in Latin America. Its ideology is rooted in Marxist-Leninist philosophy as interpreted by the Communist Party of the Soviet Union. By pursuing a gradualist, "peaceful" road to power, with formidable appeal in labor and intellectual circles, Chilean Communism has maintained its strength consistently. The Socialist Party, which emerged in the early 1930's, is also a strong and influential political force among Chilean workers. Labelling itself as Marxist, revolutionary, anticapitalist, antiimperialist, and class oriented, it occupies the left end of the political continuum. Asserting the necessity of eliminating the liberal democratic system, it advocates in its stead the establishment of a new order, authoritarian in nature but based on wide popular support.

The Christian Democratic Party, the newest of the political forces being described, occupies the left position of the Chilean Center and constitutes today the largest single electoral force in the country. Strongly influenced in its beginnings by the Belgian movement known as Rexism, it later developed a lively religious and democratic idealism, becoming populist in nature and fundamentally Christian in philosophy. The essence of its philosophy is the belief in social pluralism and political democracy. Chilean Christian Democrats, attacking the evils of communism and capitalism, developed a conception of a "middle way," which consists of the involvement of the worker in management and ownership, the promotion of intermediate groups between the state and the citizen, and government action to limit the power of large economic concentrations. Deeply influenced by the social papal encyclicals and by the thought of the French Christian philosopher Jacques Maritain, the Chilean Christian Democrats have roots that are clearly European. In advocating what they term the "communitarian society," inspired by Maritain's formulas of "a community of free men" and by Giuseppe Toniolo's idea of "a community of communities," they agree with Marx that private capital is the root of nearly every evil, and they support the abolition of private ownership of all property except consumer goods. As explained by Jaime Castillo, one of the principal party theoreticians, the political and social organization of the communitarian society would consist of a multiplicity of organizations, which can bring a greater possibility of realizing freedom than if society is simply reduced to a single social segment.[5] However, Castillo fails to go further into the structure of communitarian society. His attitude reflects the bitter ideological dispute that exists today within the Christian Democratic Party, which is the subject of this paper. This dispute is centered over whether communitarianism is to remain only an ideal vision of the society of the future or become the basis for immediate and radical reform measures restructuring property relationships in business and industry.

At this point, it must be noted that the development of Christian Democratic philosophy has never been directed by one single party ideologist. Quite the contrary, it has been the product of the influence of several figures, exerted through distinct periods, namely, Manuel Garretón, Bernardo Leighton, Radomiro Tomic, Eduardo Frei, Jaime Castillo, Jacques Chonchol, Julio Silva Solar, Bosco Parra, and others. This is consistent with Chilean tradition, since, as we have noted before, the nation's thinkers, rather than contributing original systems of philosophy, have tended to interpret foreign thought, sometimes seeking to alter European formulas to fit the special situation and the most pressing problems of the country.

However, in spite of the deep-seated pragmatism so characteristic of the Chilean political milieu, a significant departure from it is noticeable in the traditional approach to governmental problems. There is a disposition on the part of the Chilean Christian Democrats in dealing with national problems to take into account all social, economic, and political aspects of each issue through comprehensive planning of all national activities within an ideological context. Regardless of the relative ambiguity of such terms as the "communitarian society" and "economic humanism," they have, nevertheless, an ideological commitment and an essential belief in social pluralism and political democracy. The political style of the Christian Democrats, characterized by organizational efforts to involve as representative a cross section as possible of social groups in the service of a "national cause," is, at least in part, a consequence of their determination to preserve their ideological purity by closing the door to alliances with any other party or group of parties. Again, to illustrate the importance of ideology, philosophical differences among the opposition parties concerning national issues have also strengthened the independent position of the Christian Democrats.

The internal cohesion and discipline that have characterized the Chilean Christian Democratic Party since its inception have weakened, and dangerous fissures have recently appeared within its ranks. Aside from the tensions always inherent in any movement representative of a cross section of society, a number of events have recently combined to precipitate what may be called, and rightly so, a "crisis" in party affairs.

After the sweeping electoral victories of 1964 and 1965, the results of the municipal elections of April, 1967, showed a decline in party strength from its all-time high of 56 per cent of the vote in 1964 to 35.6 per cent. Although these elections, like all municipal contests, were strongly influenced by local issues, the fact remained that Frei had made a serious political miscalculation. Misled by the findings of pollsters, which had overemphasized his personal popularity after the Senate's rejection of his projected state visit to the United States, Frei had launched a vigorous personal campaign and had led the party into converting those elections into a national plebiscite. Failing to obtain the expected popular support, the party became restless, and its top-level leadership took action to determine what was to be done. A Technical-Political Committee was set up to reevaluate the 1964 platform and to suggest revisions within a two-month period.[6]

The committee, dominated by the Leftist wing of the Party, submitted a new program embodying the so-called "noncapitalist" way, which included proposals for drastic reform as well as suggestions to replace a number of cabinet members. The Committee's report was received with strong criticisms by the more moderate segment of the Party. The chief spokesman of the moderates, Senator Patricio Aylwin, then president of the Party, described the report as a slightly modified version of a communistic organization of society.[7] The leftist wing responded with new attacks upon the government's cautious and vacillating policies. At a reorganization meeting of the Party held in July, 1967, the leftist segment, led by the highly respected leader Rafael Gumucio, obtained an impressive victory over the moderates, securing control of the Party's top-level body, the National Council. This historic assembly brought into the open the rift between President Frei and large segments of the Party. A few minor political skirmishes were followed by a stalemate, which was broken when the administration introduced in Congress a proposal for a forced-savings system. The proposal was rejected by almost the entire labor sector, as well as by the majority of the leadership, of the Christian Democratic Party itself. Dissatisfaction among the Party's rank and file was augmented by the defeat of the Christian Democratic candidate at the hands of a coalition of the radical and the leftist FRAP Parties in a special senatorial election in Southern Chile. A showdown became inevitable, and it took place in early January, 1968, at a meeting of the Junta Nacional, the supreme organ of the Party, held in Peñaflor, near the capital. Determined to stamp out the revolt, President Frei made a dramatic appearance, castigated the rebels for undermining the administration, implied that they were being used by the Communists, and demanded submission. The result was only a partial victory for the President. Gumucio resigned and Jaime Castillo was elected the new president of the Party. With him other close associates of Frei returned to key party positions. But at the same time, the program embodying the "noncapitalist" way advocated by the rebel group was not officially discarded. The present situation can best be described as characterized by an uneasy truce between the factions into which the Christian Democratic Party is now divided, while the strains and tensions remain unmitigated. The proposed forced-savings law, although approved by the Chamber of Deputies by a slight majority, was rejected by the Senate's Finance Committee, an event which precipitated a cabinet crisis and the consequent removal of several ministers in early March of 1968.

The rise to power of the Christian Democratic Party created great hope that Chile would finally take the road to modernity by peaceful revolution. It was hoped that the implementation of the nationalistic, reform-oriented program of Christian Democracy would give Chile self-sustained growth to remedy its traditionally stagnant economy. Their "Revolution in Freedom," hailed as the democratic alternative to the Cuban Revolution and as a model for Latin America, has not yet fully met the new wave of hope and expectation.

An objective appraisal would clearly indicate that the achievements of the Frei administration are many. Among them are the "Chileanization" of foreign investments and important advances in agrarian reform, housing, labor organization, foreign affairs, and above all in education. But the country continues to be harrassed by the scourge of inflation and other economic problems, and many of the imponderable institutional and organizational handicaps that have shackled Chile's development remain intact. The tendency of foreign observers has been to put the blame for the slow pace of reform on the obstructionism of opposition parties, and their criticism has seldom been directed to the Christian Democrats themselves. If it is true that the opposition of the parties of the Right as well as of the Left has held firmly since the

Christian Democrats took power and that the Senate has been
the chief obstruction to Frei's proposals, it is equally true that
failure to push forward his measures is due, at least in part,
to lack of effective leadership and/or unwillingness or inabili-
ty on the part of the Christian Democrats to negotiate and
compromise.

To all this one must add that much of the administration's
inefficiency in implementing reforms can be ascribed to internal differences within the Party. The causes for dissension
are often related to the lack of strong leadership on the part
of the chief executive. President Frei has had multiple opportunities to take firm control of the Party. Instead he has
chosen to remain aloof, a figure above politics, resorting to
party support only when the pressure of the opposition becomes too strong. Present internal strains have revealed the
existence of at least three distinct party groupings, whose
goals and objectives often conflict among themselves as well
as with those of the government. One is the so-called neocapitalist group. Composed of influential industrialists and
businessmen, who are linked to the traditional financial interests, this faction is in general loyal to Frei but would like
his administration to adopt a more moderate line toward business. It favors control of inflation through monetary and fiscal
policies, a check on salary and wage increases, and less taxation. Naturally, this group puts great emphasis on the protection of private enterprise and seeks promotion of those
activities that can offer greater opportunities to private enterprise. A second group is that of the centrists or middle-of-the
roaders. Their members, including many of the Party found-
ers, share an intense personal loyalty to Frei and are lending
him unconditional support. Ideologically, they maintain the
postulates of Frei's presidential platform of 1964. Representing the old guard of the original movement and the early
party organization, the Falange Nacional, they occupy most

ministerial positions and high-level bureaucratic posts, and they are also well represented in both houses of the Congress.

The third group, constituting the left wing, is chiefly composed of the youngest elements in the party and a small group of prestigious national leaders who are strongly committed to the Christian Democratic philosophy. This segment advocates rapid implementation of the 1964 program through the application of the "noncapitalist" formula for development, which would lead to the establishment of the "communitarian society." The increasing use of the term "communitarian socialism" by this left wing, specially by the youth organizations that constitute its core, is indicative of its opposition to the survival of "capitalist" property relationships in the country.

The principal objectives which this group maintains can be successfully achieved through its "noncapitalist" approach to developmental problems include: (1) acceleration of Chile's rate of economic growth; (2) decrease in the country's economic dependence on foreign nations; (3) fairer distribution of the national income; (4) increasing popular participation in public affairs; and (5) democratization of the socioeconomic system and the power structure of the country. Complementary goals are a high level of employment and monetary stabilization. Implied in the "noncapitalist" formula are some basic notions: The state must act as the basic dynamic force in the developmental process through the effective use of all control mechanisms. The Chilean economy must be "democratized" and the traditional alliance between great financial powers and industry must be broken. Areas of activity and the "rules of the game" delineating the proper spheres of action for both the public and the private sectors of the economy must be established and observed. A clearly defined system of priorities for the allocation of financial resources to be used for developmental activities, which would give emphasis to agrarian reform, must be adopted. Among the most urgent tasks is that of organizing intermediate structures capable of articulating popular demands and of assuring effective mass participation in governmental planning.[8]

It is too early to predict whether the present schism in Christian Democratic ranks between the ideologically committed and the pragmatically inclined will lead to an irrevocable party division or to significant doctrinal shifts. It may well be that the fate reserved for the party is the same as that suffered by the Radical Party, which, prior to the rise of Christian Democracy, occupied the center of the Chilean political spectrum exclusively. In the course of its long history, the Radical Party veered at times to the right, pushed by those within its fold who responded to traditional interests. At other times, it was impelled to the left under pressure from its Marxist-oriented segments. Although the split personality of the Radical Party saved it from dangerous extremism, its dependence on coalition politics jeopardized the party's future, because, as circumstances changed, the cost of dependence for support on either rightist or leftist groups resulted in vague ideology and in hollow and expedient programs, and eventually in serious deterioration of its electoral strength.

Actually, the three Christian Democratic factions which have been described are fairly representative of the informal coalition of sorts that carried them to power in 1964. Special circumstances that year impelled the rightist forces to throw their unconditional support to Frei. Long before this time progressive-minded dissidents from the conservatives had gradually swelled Christian Democratic ranks, and the party had moved slowly to the center in order to broaden its popular base. After attracting many formerly orthodox leftist intellectuals in the late 1940's, the party then began moving to the center and the right for additional support. Naturally, the rightist newcomers began to exert influence upon party leadership. By the time of the 1964 election the party had ceased to be the small but highly homogenous and disciplined organization that entered the political arena in 1938. It had become a cross section of various groups, often with conflicting interests. Thus, the "newcomers," who were essentially advocates of a conservative position, are now represented by the "neocapitalist" group within the Party, and, lacking personal bonds and a firm ideological attachment to the Party, they are the most likely to desert it under trying circumstances. The Centrists, representing many of the Party's founding fathers and the hard core of the present administration, constitute the nucleus of a moderate bloc that supports a truly national government representing all Chileans and serving the "national cause." Confronted with the crude reality of governing and often instinctively moved by Chilean pragmatism, the Centrists are trying to shape their policies so as not to drive the opposition to extremes. The left wing, representative of the ideologically highly committed and zealous party youth, is concerned with the cautiousness of the old guard leadership and fearful of a possible sell-out of the revolutionary aspects of the "communitarian ideal."

The dilemma that this poses for the Christian Democrats is, if anything, more difficult than the one confronted by the Radicals in the past. The very nature and composition of the Radical Party since its inception made it possible for it to undergo changes in leadership, policy, and even principle and to practice coalition politics without serious consequences. On the other hand, Christian Democratic philosophy with its neosocialistic economic and democratic political ideology, in contrast to the undefined ideology of Chilean Radicalism, has always been the *raison d'etre* of the Party. And yet it could be ventured that, given the nature of the Chilean political system, characterized as it is by a multiparty system composed of organizations representing the entire range of political tendencies, it is an almost insurmountable task for a party to dominate the political field and at the same time preserve its ideological purity. The pattern of "coalition politics" established as a result of the emergence of new political forces in the last three decades may be too deeply rooted to permit such domination by a single political force.

Notes

[1] "The Role of Popular Organizations in the State," excerpt from *Primer Mensaje del Presidente de la República de Chile al Congreso Nacional* (May 21, 1965), published by the Presidential Department of Publications, Santiago; trans. by the editor. In *The Ideologies of the Developing Nations*, Rev. ed., ed. Paul E. Sigmund (New York, 1967), p. 391.

[2] Among them Eduardo Frei of Chile.

[3] Federico G. Gil, *The Political System of Chile* (Boston, 1966), pp. 244–245.

[4] Gil, *The Political System of Chile*, pp. 257–266.

[5] Jaime Castillo, "Property and the Communitarian Society," in *The Ideologies of the Developing Nations*, ed. Paul E. Sigmund, pp. 400–404.

[6] This committee was composed of Jacques Chonchol as president and Tomás Reyes, Luis Maira, Vincente Sotta, Julio Silva, Carlos Massad, and Pedro Felipe Ramírez. All its members occupied important positions in the administration or in the Congress.

[7] Patricio Aylwin, "Discordia de las vías," *Ercilla*, No. 1690 (October 25, 1967), p. 5.

[8] *Presente*, No. 2 (July 14, 1967), p. 2.

Oyama Cesar Ituassú da Silva

International Institutions for Development*

IN EVERYTHING there is a historical phase which influences events, including the theme of this paper. But which socio-historical periods paved the way for and still influence the modification of ever-present self-interest—the common denominator of all conflicts?

There are three levels in mankind's struggle for better living conditions: *man, society,* and *community,* each one representing a hard and difficult stage, achieved with a tenacity that only self-interest, in the best sense of the word, could supply.

When the first two human beings met each other, the first *development* emerged through need for survival; but it appeared under the specific guise of individualism because neither person admitted a material superiority on the part of the other. Man, a thinking animal, later understood that he could and should function more efficiently if he were to join with others; and the strongest or the most skillful assumed leadership, so as to permit through the resulting evolution the political birth of the state.

The state, absolute and absolutist, preserved and enhanced the selfish character of its citizens; and in subsequent periods it pursued ruthlessly its needs and objectives, all under the

* This article is a slightly abridged version of the paper given by Oyama Cesar Ituassú da Silva at the SECOLAS. It appeared in Portuguese in the *Journal of Inter-American Studies*, Vol. 10, No. 3 (July, 1968), pp. 431–42.

guise of a specified advancement. This situation prevailed until, in our era, an inner spark of enlightenment became visible.

The fact is that the understanding of interdependence, in the sense that nobody can live and progress by himself, created a new mentality, that of *international community*, consisting of the principle of the common relationship of all beings—corporate or physical—having in view a common goal. The concept of community expresses the idea that all must live in such a way that living becomes more harmonious and better adjusted; thus life reaches its fulfillment.

One can see that the traditional assumptions, which originated from political power for self-aggrandizement and resulted in the impoverishment of the other coparticipants of international life, lost ground to the idea of social adjustment, causing both the disruption of established mechanisms for private control and the subversion of social values. This process has been called the "process of secularization," in which the old powers, facing the change of social structure, still offer resistance to the attitudes of newer generations.

So it happens that "secularization" is manifested as a result of progress, and this fact has more than economic significance; it is visible in the panoramas of structural change in the contemporary world. These changes have been derived from three principal phenomena: the *technological process*, an expression of the material evolution of the machine and the consequent liberation of man from the social slavery in which until then he had found himself, only to pass, in a certain sense, to a new type of slavery conceived and executed by the state; the *demographic process*, resulting from the ease and comfort of modern life and longer life expectancy, which permits uncontrolled growth of populations; and the *ecological process*, a product of the first two, requiring more complex activity on the part of the people.

The new combination of historical events and processes produces a better adjustment of the various conflicting interests and an inevitable interrelationship among them, culminating in an objectively considered reality. This reality, notwithstanding the narrow egocentrism of the state, has become an international political problem. Politics, within its proper context, aims to benefit all groups through better support of public causes, and it cannot avoid development as a response to the need for individual advancement, the starting point for collective evolution.

Development should be considered not only in its economic content but, more importantly, in its idealistic meaning of ethical-juridical purpose, since this concept is involved in its basic nature. Development is progress in a broad sense and it especially concerns juridical decisions. There is progress only when, along with the economic, financial, cultural, and social movements, there is also a broadening of juridical values, permitting a greater equilibrium in the domestic or international collective life.

There is, therefore, a perceptible difference between *development* and *civilization*; the former expresses the sum of progressive movements in general, while the latter, linked more to the concepts of the moment, involves only a step in the long evolutionary ladder. Civilization is a concept, whereas development is an upward movement. The great civilizations of the past—Persian, Etruscan, Egyptian, Mayan, Aztecan, Incan, etc.—each expressed in its passage only one phase without having resulted in development. They indicated only a historical level in development. The latter, therefore, is more closely related to evolution, the successive steps in progress and refinement of societies and their civilizations.

The particular self-interest of each state finally gave way to the collective interest by reason of the world crises of this century. Men unite themselves only in critical moments in history, searching for a common solution to their problems and their sufferings. And the crises of this era favored the emergence of new pressures for change in the prevailing attitudes that had previously dominated civilization in general and, above all, the so-called western culture. The despair and confusion of man—who sees himself disoriented and lost in a world of disorder lacking in high ideals and full of contrasts and unrest—has made imperative the substantial modification of the existing systems in order to avoid disaster and chaos.

Truly, the transformation of the contemporary world has occurred because peculiar circumstances profoundly disturbed the equilibrium of the prewar and postwar worlds. The secularization of culture and of life, with the disregard of moral problems and the failure to solve them, the absence of genuine cultural elites, together with the disparagement of professions of a spiritual nature, the acceleration of the use of technology and machines, the destruction of the middle class which until this century has constituted the balancing point of societies, the collision of antagonistic classes along with the establishment of the slogans *bourgeoisie* and *proletariat*, the excessive accumulation of people around cities, the abandonment of the traditional rural life, which had always preserved national economic reserves and always been the mainstay of societies, resulting in the decline of agricultural production—all these factors were instrumental in the transformation. To this imposing set of facts should be added the state's self-worship, which, based on military and industrial power, has nullified the current ideas of administration of public affairs and made the state a kind of corporation manager intervening and interfering in economic life. All these socio-politico-economic elements created the urgent need for total reform of the enfeebled organism of the international community in order to prevent its sinking in a morass of confused claims.

All development involves transition, and the intermediate stages soften the blow of the breaking up of old structures harmful to the new social order, and thus permit the union of the various interests in such a way as not to create too many frictions between its components. There must be considered, as Gino Germani indicates,[1] the peculiar aspects of the modern transformation, which are:

    a—modification of the types of social action
    b—institutionalization of the component transformations
    c—specialization of the institutions.

These are sociological subjects, it is true, but they have fundamental importance in the problem under study. The curtailment of opportunities through specialization narrows the individual horizon and imperils the common welfare, which is the catalyst of social evolution. It is necessary to break the restrictions imposed upon freedom of choice in order to stimulate man to discover new fields of work and thus to widen the professional horizons. The machine is gradually taking the place of human activity; and manual labor is affected by this substitution, becoming less valuable and, among many, even contemptible. It is necessary that quality regain its prevalence over quantity, without disrupting, however, the importance of volume, which is essential to supply the demands and needs of world markets.

All social change implies a change of attitude. This observation was made by Professor Orlando Gomes (*Direito e Desenvolvimento*, p. 19).[2] He also tells us that "the social process seeks its discipline in a new system of norms," and the juridical decree constitutes, "as it regulates the conduct of men and of society, the principal influence in the process of development," making manifest the "institutionalization of the transformations." It is understood that law is not merely a set of rules but a social entity; its action has repercussions in all sectors of human life, as a touchstone for evaluating existential relationships.

It must also be kept in mind that transformations produce

new criteria of specialization of activities which institutions cannot disregard. Social diversification requires that the processes that reshape political thought, if linked to the collective well-being, tend to become specialized in order to better accomplish their objectives. But all the changes do not take place in parallel or in identical rhythm. World-wide variations of attitudes, ingrained beliefs, and political criteria, and local delays in development—levels in the evolutionary process— are important factors that make difficult the synchronization of planned action. The multiplicity of these factors and the diversity of the world's needs therefore require specialization as a means of accelerating the rate of progress of mankind.

The adoption of new criteria demonstrates that the essence of civilization is increased recognition that there are alternative solutions for social problems and opportunity to explore new solutions, as Quincy Wright indicates.[3] Our century is moving rapidly towards a better understanding of the evolutionary stage we have reached, and the traditional opposition can no longer nullify the human quality of mutual understanding. Man opens his own inner way to this understanding at the cost of vast sacrifices and sufferings, and learns day by day, in disquietude and in suffering, the bitter lesson. The damage that has resulted from an uncontrolled rate of population increase in densely populated regions, and the availability of better solutions—better opportunities for those who attempt to progress—has stimulated the application of new methods of finding and utilizing alternate solutions.

The dependence on the balance of power that existed during the last two centuries has been overcome. This period did, however, assure the emergence of the embryonic international community, even though based in a firm oligarchy. The Holy Alliance was such an oligarchy; it usurped, in a kind of officious international management of business, the right to guide and manage collective life, as Jiménez de Aréchaga states in *Derecho Constitucional de las Naciones Unidas*.[4]

Incredible as it may seem, however, the treaty of absolutist control of September 26, 1815, which created the Holy
Alliance, contains in the main the original principle of development in clauses which the contracting powers saw fit to
renew:

> ... meetings consecrated to the large interests and to the exam-
> ination of measures that in each of these eras may be judged
> more healthful for the rest and prosperity of the peoples and
> for the maintenance of peace in Europe.

Certainly, it was not yet a question of an agreement for international aid; what resulted were collective proceedings
which the participants decided to introduce into the practical
politics of the states. In any event, the statement expressed a
tendency toward the better, although the nations continued
to be under the aegis of the sovereigns of the period, imbued
with all the privileges and prejudices of the age.

The error of the Holy Alliance lay in attempting development within a political system, because development is necessarily contrary to any activity of a political nature; therefore,
the hostile influences inherent in the individualistic bent of
the states would render ineffective and useless any measures
that by chance might be taken. However, the Holy Alliance
did contribute its share of idealism in such a way as to provide
foundations for future plans of accomplishment by the international community and to make its intentions realizable in
the future.

Such precedents created a climate, in the second stage, for
the awakening of the common conscience to progress, evidenced by the Pact of the League of Nations in 1919, whose
aim of universality could not disregard the problem of development. But the Pact, because it was the result of one war
and the smouldering ruins of the conflict still stirred the minds
of the conferees, took special care to set up an international
organization to prevent and combat wars and to strengthen

nascent political institutions. However, it paid little attention to the central and most important question—the progress of the people. Certainly the oligarchic or autocratic mentality of the new collective government—with the great powers predominating as the ruling class—jeopardized the cause of development within a specialized system of social transformation. It is only in the last thirty years that efforts have been made to make a methodical analysis of the question—the progress of the people—from the meeting of the International Monetary and Economic Conference of 1933 to study and solve various problems related to production and underdevelopment. At this conference the brilliant and lucid spirit of Frank McDougall, the representative of Australia, stood out. His goal was the creation of an international organization to study these crucial matters, but he was unsuccessful, in spite of his incomparable faith and perseverence. However, his dream was eventually realized in the Food and Agriculture Organization.

That, however, came only after World War II, with the almost total destruction of Europe, which accentuated the necessity of substantial specialized aid to the countries affected by the war. The UNRRA (United Nations Recovery and Rehabilitation Administration) also emerged as the agency charged with the task—already designated in the sixth article of the Atlantic Charter of August 14, 1941—of giving "every man of every land the security of being able to live free from want and hunger." This agency, with tenacity and fabulous resources, made possible the recovery of the continent. Today Europe, now that UNRRA's mission has been accomplished, is a prosperous area dedicated to work and progress.

The forward drive continued with the meeting of the Hot Springs Conference of 1943, dedicated to food and agriculture. This conference led directly to the foundation, on October 16, 1945, of the United Nations Food and Agriculture

Organization (FAO), which has spread its dynamic and efficient action far and wide, concentrating on hunger. Hunger, the antagonist which menaces all mankind, found in that organization a determined opponent which, little by little, despite the stumbling blocks and obstacles, is overcoming its most urgent aspects.

The dreams of men found temporary shelter in the United Nations, the Charter of which reads:

> We, the peoples of the United Nations, determined . . . to promote social progress and better standards of life in larger freedom, and for these ends . . . *to employ international machinery for the promotion of the economic and social advancement of all peoples* [italics are Itaussú's], have resolved to combine our efforts to accomplish these aims.

In these words, the Charter stated the firm intention of promoting international cooperation to solve economic, social, cultural, and humanitarian problems. It accomplished much through the Economic and Social Welfare Council, which has the function of overseeing and coordinating development, as stipulated in Articles 55 and 62. Thus the evolution of mankind reached the stage of specialized international institutions, which resulted from the states' centering their attention on one common ideal.

The Conference of the Afro-Asian States, held in Bandung from April 14 to 25, 1955, emphasized in its final communiqué the importance of international aid for development and pointed out the necessity of establishing a fund of the United Nations for that purpose. It proclaimed its conviction that friendly cooperation in accordance with the principles of freedom will contribute effectively to the maintenance and consolidation of peace and security, and also that cooperation in the economic, social, and cultural fields will contribute to the prosperity and welfare of all.

An analysis of the facts indicates a breakdown of the institutions for development into the following categories:

a—economic institutions
b—commercial institutions
c—political institutions
d—structural institutions.

Each allows valuable contributions from the community of peoples and nations, even though the four types may have different specific goals.

One cannot deny that economic and commercial self-interests adjust and adapt themselves when motivated by a common interest. But although economic and commercial institutions may have a profound effect on the process of development, they do not assume a distinctive or supreme role because evolution is effected more through basic reforms, which are recognized for their own merit. Institutions that are primarily commercial, like the European Common Market and the Latin American Free Trade Association, with identical objectives, intend to establish a single system of interests within restricted international activity with regional objectives. Yet these objectives definitely contribute to general development.

The political factors, however, must be linked to the structural features that determine the social regulation of the various groups within the objective of elevating man in himself and as an integral part of an organized body politic to the point that everyone may enjoy well-being and peace. Obviously, the political pact that created BENELUX on October 28, 1947, under the form of a customs union uniting Belgium, Holland, and Luxembourg as a customs community, expresses an evolutionary process in international relations that is contributive to development. In a like manner, the European Organization of Economic Cooperation, created on April 16,

1948, and having as its goal a common program of continental development, also offers a vast potential for the planned guidance of general progress.

By contrast, there is another kind of specialized political institution that is concerned only with ideological aspects of the historical picture which is being attempted. Such institutions, because of the closed circle in which they function, contribute very little to the solution of the problem of development. They are dedicated almost exclusively to plans of domination, to the detriment of the large and superior community interests. Examples of this type of political institution exist in the North Atlantic Treaty Organization—NATO—and the Southeast Asia Treaty Organization—SEATO—the aims of which are simply the territorial defense of the areas in which they are concerned against the threat of ideologically hostile states. Such organizations limit their activities chiefly to organizing destruction—not progress and development. (This explains why it is that Europe, civilized as it is, has still not learned, even after centuries of political life, how to advance by way of collective action. The same is true of the Slavic and Asian peoples in their fight to gain world supremacy—a fight that has been repeatedly attempted by many and defeated.)

The high point, however, of institutions of all kinds is found in those which work for the structural improvement of the whole society of peoples and states. These structural institutions are devoted to the premise that only progress shared by all will provide opportunity for the peaceful coexistence that is necessary for the desired economic and social welfare. (The humane expression of this premise is the International Red Cross, a realization of the dreams of Moynier and Dunant, but it is not enough to keep man happy on earth.)

Such structural organizations are the United Nations, the Organization of American States, and the new African Unity

Pact, signed in Addis Ababa on May 15, 1963. All of them, without exception, have endorsed the high goals of mutual understanding and aid because only the collective effort for the benefit of all can give man and society what they desire: peace to produce, peace to think of the future, and peace to accomplish goals. The United Nations, as we have already said, adopted the basic rule of full cooperation to attain social peace through common progress in the economic, cultural, public health, and other fields, and this rule is institutionalized in FAO, UNESCO, and WHO.

The American continent could not remain uninvolved in collective development, because it includes both extremes of the problem under study: at one extreme, a powerful, developed state (which deviated from its historic course to enter the race for world power); and at the other extreme, the other nations of the continent, which arrived in an inferior station by reason of inhibiting circumstances. Despite its resources, the continent has not been able to achieve the necessary material development. The so-called western civilization has not yet reached every corner of this hemisphere, nor has modern technology managed to exploit the economic resources in directions consistent with the needs of the populations. But perhaps because of the lack of less relevant ambitions, the American states advanced rapidly in the establishment of institutions for progress. And the OAS is unsurpassed among structural institutions, by reason of its formulation of juridical principles of collective conduct.

The Charter of the Organization of American States declared:

> Social justice and social security are bases of lasting peace.
> i) Economic cooperation is essential to the common welfare and prosperity of the peoples of the continent.

At the same time, the Charter establishes economic and social criteria, consistent with the overall spirit of good neighbors, for improving the general economy—agriculture, industry, and commerce—and, especially, for mutual cooperation for the good of the population. It also stresses the right of all people to education.

One sees, then, that the American States, even though the overwhelming majority of them are underdeveloped, have espoused, within the system of the Organization, the concept of mutual aid for the solution of common problems. (Its predecessor, the Pan-American Union, had already rendered some services of this nature, working for the welfare of the community through improvement of public health throughout the continent.) Further, the Organization gives first priority to respect for man's individuality as a condition of his interdependence, as is evident in the following clauses:

—The rights of each state depend not upon its power to ensure the exercise thereof, but upon the mere fact of its existence . . .

—The right of each State to protect itself and to live its own life does not authorize it to commit unjust acts against another State.

—The spiritual unity of the continent is based on respect for the cultural values of the American countries and requires their close cooperation for the high purposes of civilization.

—The education of peoples should be directed toward justice, freedom and peace.

The Organization of American States follows faithfully its original fundamental ideas. These ideas, because of their purity, have also been reflected in the recent Pact of African Unity, whose Article 2 states forcefully the intentions of "coordinating and intensifying their efforts and collaboration, for the purpose of gaining a better life for the peoples of Africa."

All these postulates were derived from the prominent character of the American peoples, and this continent initiated the general coordination of developmental policy. In the purely juridical area, both America and Africa proclaimed continental solidarity and arbitration as safe and firm bases from which to attack their problems. Ahead of their time, both organizations testify to the evolutionary nature of their temperament and spirit. From them we can conclude that civilization is not synonymous with evolution. There are civilized and developed peoples who have not evolved spiritually, while others, less fortunate materially, possess a profound sense of spirituality.

From these examples it is clear that development and law are intermingled and interconnected. It is impossible to conceive of progress without juridical stimulus because change in social norms inevitably involves change of structure. And only change of structure, supported by law, can produce lasting effects.

The modern world exhibits a panorama of social maladjustment. Some states attempt domination of others by economic processes, and others rely on subjugation. The great majority of nations—especially those of Latin America and Black Africa—suffer the pernicious handicap of a deficiency of essential elements for development—complete lack of almost everything. Their great human masses are tired of suffering from hunger and of enduring miseries and hardships. It has become difficult for the powerful states to ignore them and their needs and the reality of interdependence among the states, small and large. The large states, within structurally specialized organizations, have to establish firm programs for the progressive elevation of less favored countries in order to guarantee themselves a more tranquil and better life.

What is happening in the world today, full of uncertainty and restlessness, is the logical result of the blindness that so long afflicted those responsible for the destiny of the world. But by now we have learned that no process of reform can long survive if it is not supported by a juridical structure that is the manifestation of the change in social standards and objectives. Development without law is an aberration. Law, without concomitant development, is socially useless. Orlando Gomes crystalizes the lesson in the observation:

> The risk of social disintegration can be avoided, or at least diminished, if institutions are modified, gradually, through an intelligent policy, of which reform of juridical institutions is a part.[5]

Notes

[1] Gino Germani, "Secularization, Modernization, and Economic Development," in *The Protestant Ethic and Modernization*, ed. by S. N. Eisenstadt (New York, 1968), p. 345. [This chapter, pp. 343–366, is a revised version of an essay published in *Resistência a Mudança* (Rio de Janeiro, 1960).]

[2] Orlando Gomes, *Direito e Desenvolvimento* (Bahia, 1961), p. 19.

[3] Quincy Wright, *A Study of War*, abridged ed. (Chicago, 1964), p. 426.

[4] Eduardo Jiménez de Aréchaga, *Derecho Constitucional de las Naciones Unidas* (Madrid, 1958), pp. 12–19.

[5] Gomes, *Direito e Desenvolvimento*, pp. 26–27.

INDEX OF PROPER NAMES